WILDFIRE THROUGH STAFFORDSHIRE

Published by Mapseeker Archive Publishing Ltd, Mapseeker Studio, 30 High Street, Aldridge, Walsall, WS9 8LZ, Tel: +44 (0) 1922 288111 / +44 (0)1922 458288

Printed by Butler Tanner & Dennis, Caxton Road, Frome, Somerset, BA11 1NF, +44 (0)1373 451500

British Library Cataloguing in Publication Data.
A catalogue record for this book is available from the British Library.

ISBN 978-1-84491-797-6 Hardcover

Typesetting and design by Adrian Baggett
Cover design by Emily Benton

Historical maps available to buy at
www.mapseeker.co.uk

PUBLISHED
& PRINTED
IN ENGLAND

MAPSEEKER
ARCHIVE • PUBLISHING
GATEWAY TO OUR HISTORIC PAST
www.mapseeker.co.uk

WILDFIRE THROUGH STAFFORDSHIRE

PAUL LESLIE LINE
&
MATT LANGHAM

FOREWORD BY MICHAEL PEARSON

POEMS BY IAN HENERY

ILLUSTRATED BY ADRIAN BAGGETT

MAPSEEKER ARCHIVE PUBLISHING

FOREWORD

I was delighted when Mapseeker invited me to write the foreword for this book. The material they publish is of the highest standard, with quality artwork, interesting subject matter, but most impressive is their final production, with some of the best quality books in their class I have had the pleasure to read. You will enjoy the rich colourisation of the maps and accompanying artwork, liberally sprinkled throughout. Every turn of the page will deliver another course in this banquet of sumptuous imagery. The accompanying text of the journey comes from the Osborne Guide. It was one of several guides of its day, and is contemporary with George Bradshaw's more famous, but more general, railway guide. Poetry is supplied by Ian Henery, Walsall Poet Laureate, a prolific poet who frequently writes of his Black Country ancestors and life in the Black Country

The subject of this book is that of a railway journey on a single railway line, rather than Bradshaw's more general guide.It begins in Birmingham near Aston Church and viaduct, passes through Warwickshire and parts of Staffordshire, including the western parts of the Black Country (or the 'Iron District' as it was then known), and on into Cheshire, before connecting with the Liverpool and Manchester Railway to complete the journey.

The book is a comprehensive account of this journey as far as the Cheshire border and the narrative paints a vivid picture of this journey as the trains weaves it way north and west. The period is at the start of the Railway Age (1830–1914) and is probably the most significant railway in the early Victorian period; it joined four regions, each with growing industrial capacity: Birmingham, the Black Country, Liverpool, providing access to the world, and finally Manchester. In modern terms, this railway was the equivalent of the 21st Century HS2 high-speed rail link.

What makes this book stand out is the 'vehicle' which is used to traverse the Grand Junction Railway; without the 'Wildfire' the book would be more of a mere travel guide and less of a story of a great journey. This is a book to be admired, perhaps to be read in advance of a similar journey, so you, the traveller/reader can gain an insight into its history and significance to Britain and the Empire. You are fortunate, should you wish to undertake this journey, because the lines used in the 1840s are still in existence today and so you can recreate the journey, though sadly not by steam. Enjoy!

Michael Pearson 2014

ACKNOWLEDGEMENTS

I would like to express my grateful thanks to everyone who has contributed to making this publication possible and those who have spent many hours passionately applying their skills and expertise, reflected in the completed work, with special thanks to the following.

Matt Langham for his authorial contribution in the creation of "The Journey" from the original accounts, Mike Pearson for kindly writing the Foreword, and David Moore for writing the introduction.

Adrian Baggett for his illustrative skills and book design throughout and also Emily Benton in the early design of the cover; Steve Toulouse and Phil Bradney for their many hours of meticulous and painstaking work digitally re-creating the many antique original antique town plans, views and vistas featured in this publication.

Berian Williams and Steve Bartrick for sourcing additional antique views and vistas used in the book and Lynn Hughes, artist, for her wonderful pencil and charcoal drawings, courtesy of Mary Evans Picture library, in the section "Visiting the South Staffordshire Mining and Manufacturing District 1838".

Stuart Williams for providing the central Willenhall section of Beckett's Poor Rate Plan, courtesy of Walsall Local History Centre, used as the base for the "Map of Willenhall 1838".

Ed Bartholomew from the National Railway Museum for the information provided about the Wildfire Engine featured on page 144, and finally Jo Lloyd from Staffordshire County Council for providing the list of up to date visitor attractions across Staffordshire – "The Creative County".

Paul Leslie Line 2014
Mapseeker Publishing Ltd

INTRODUCTION

The Grand Junction Railway was one of the very first long distance railways in the world to use steam locomotives. Previous long distance lines like Cromford and High Peak Railway had originally been horse drawn tramways.

The line was authorised by Parliament in 1833 and designed by the engineers George Stephenson, Joseph Locke and John Rastrick. It ran for 82 miles from Birmingham through Wolverhampton, Stafford, Crewe, and Warrington. The line then joined the existing Warrington and Newton Railway to link with the cities of Liverpool and Manchester and the industrial heartlands of Birmingham and the Black Country.

This was an undertaking like no other. Its opening coincided with the birth of the Victorian era, and showcased engineering achievement at its very finest; setting a standard that many others would be inspired to follow. The newly crowned Queen Victoria would have been highly delighted, if not amused.

The line officially opened for business on 4 July 1837 with a temporary Birmingham terminus at Vauxhall, Nechells, though services were soon routed to Curzon Street in Birmingham where the company shared the station with the London and Birmingham railway. The adjacent platforms effectively provided the railway link between the cities of Manchester, Liverpool, Birmingham and London.

The Grand Junction Railway Company quickly became a highly successful organisation. So incredible was the Victorian engineers' foresight and vision, that within three years they quickly seized on the opportunity to absorb the Chester and Crewe Railway before it opened. It was this success and growth that led the Grand Junction Railway Company to build its locomotive works at Crewe which allowed Crewe to become a major railway town.

The Grand Junction Railway's long term vision was to become part of a grand northern national railway network. It actively encouraged the development of the North Union Railway which took the line onward to the northern town of Preston, while investing in the Lancaster and Carlisle Railway and the Caledonian Railway. This laid the foundation for what we now know as the central section of West Coast Main line.

Although the Grand Junction Railway was one of the very first long distance railways in the world to use steam locomotives, its initial operation was a very modest concern. When opened in 1837, a locomotive pulling three coaches and a mail train set off from Liverpool, and a similar one set off from Manchester. It was on this route that mail sorting was first carried out. The mail was processed by clerks riding in a special carriage which had a net for catching mail bags at stations without stopping. Both trains met at Newtown Junction where they were combined and hauled southward by the locomotive Wildfire to Birmingham.

Osborne's map of the Grand Junction Railway follows the route of Wildfire which was one of a series of somewhat similar 2-2-2 locomotives built by the Robert Stephenson Co and is credited with being the first locomotive working train to pass through Wolverhampton from Birmingham.

As the railway boom expanded, the railway companies were quite keen to promote their new lines and rail services. Although initially railways were built to facilitate the movement of goods, the rail companies were very quick to seize the opportunity presented by the demand of an upwardly mobile population.

This new era of the Victorian engineer marked a key point in the history of the Industrial Revolution, a phenomenon that has influenced almost every aspect

of our daily lives in some way or other. With average wages rapidly rising the population began to show signs of extraordinary growth. Nothing remotely like this economic behavior had happened before.

Commentators of the time such as Osborne, Roscoe, Wyld and Drake noticed and were clearly concerned that the increase in population had fuelled a change in the social structure too. They wrote that in the Black Country, large families became extremely common and housing conditions were predominantly poor. Water borne disease like cholera and typhoid had become increasingly common.

Osborne writes: "In the months of August and September, 1832, there were no less than 3,568 cases of cholera, and 742 deaths; so raging and fatal was the disease that neither doctors, nurses, coffins, nor graves, could be procured fast enough. Out of a population of 160,000, in the mining district, there were 10,000 cases of cholera, and nearly 2,500 deaths".

Fortunately, as the inventive Victorian engineers fuelled the growth of the industrial revolution, bringing with it the poor health and housing conditions, these very same railway engineers sought a solution to the problems that they had inadvertently created.

It was John Snow, a physician, who linked the outbreaks of cholera to contaminated water. With the water supply of the Black Country only partially satisfied by the meagre, impure sources available from a communal pump or wells, and cholera and other associated diseases causing the deaths of thousands of people, there was a dire need for an organised waterworks scheme.

The railway engineer, John Robinson McClean, who was the owner of the South Staffordshire Railway established the South Staffordshire Waterworks Company at Sandfields, Lichfield. McClean commissioned Edward Adams, an engineer, to design and build a magnificent building, adjacent to the railway line.

Adams was clearly inspired by Brunel and modelled the waterworks on his infamous South Devon Atmospheric Railway. He designed and built a magnificent Gothic revival structure that showcased the dawn of Victorian splendour, conveying to the

visitor and investor alike a sense of the longevity, creativity and attention to detail of a job well done.

The waterworks were so successful that within the space of a few years, the demand for the life-giving water had doubled, so McClean commissioned the installation of a 150 horse power Cornish beam engine. Built by Jonah and George Davies of Tipton at the time it was cutting edge technology. It pumped two million gallons of water every day, almost non-stop from 1873 to 1927, breathing life into the beleaguered communities of the Black Country.

Today, part of the original South Staffordshire Waterworks Company buildings at Sandfields are still intact, and can be seen by the side of the South Staffordshire Railway at Lichfield. A group is fighting to preserve this significant historical building and protect it for future generations so that it becomes part of the rich heritage of the Back Country and an integral part of our industrial past.

In the 1830's these early railway guides, hand books and maps became the first of an increasing number of publications which were produced as new railways opened across the country. All were eager to expound the virtues of their great railways.

Bradshaw's guide, which is the subject of a recent television series, was in fact a set of timetables, and did not contain any tourist information. The Bradshaw's Handbooks for tourists in Great Britain and Ireland were not actually published until 1860 and were a rival publication to Osborne's original Railway Guide.

The maps and guides are significant accounts of our past and give us an insight into the lives of working individuals, and tell us fascinating and remarkable stories about the people who lived and worked in the industrial towns along the route of the railways from Birmingham and the Black Country to Liverpool and Manchester. Osborne describes the landscape of Britain with a poet's eye, and at the same time paints a very accurate picture of how the countryside was undergoing social change. Osborne had a vast knowledge of history, geography and biology, which he put to use in his frequent travels on Wildfire along the route.

Osborne's Guide to the Grand Junction Railway was originally published in 1838 and is written in a prosaic form of English which has, alas, faded somewhat from our modernistic view of life. The

style of writing confided his thoughts, experiences and feeling to the written page. Other than personal diaries, no other documents offer such a wealth of information about the day to day life of the Victorian age and the ups and downs of their daily life. In recent years, there has been a terrific growth in the quest to know one's self; this has subsequently fuelled a prolific growth in people interested in their own history. The value of this publication is by understanding our own history in bringing together people's relationships with the past. By uncovering the past, we reveal a wealth of stories and histories of everyday life. These stories are both engaging people with the history and propagate a historical desire to understand more of this 'how things were'.

Copies of the original Osborne's map which were a folded insert in the guide are now quite often found in poor condition and are very rare. This new publication contains a copy of the map that has been completely and painstakingly re-constructed, restored and enhanced as well as tastefully and carefully colourised by Mapseeker Publishing. This map is now a joy to look at and read, reflecting the splendid restorative process that took over three months to complete. The book contains many attractive engravings, contemporary to the period, showcasing the line and surroundings areas, in splendid detail. The many thought provoking poems have been specially created by Ian Henery, Walsall Poet Laureate, adding a new dimension to Osborne's observations.

This guide is unparalleled in illustrating the achievements of the Victorian engineers and the Grand Junction Railway company, from the unadulterated splendour of the first class coach, to the ten arch viaduct bridging the London line. This is indeed the ultimate armchair guide.

The lines which made up the Grand Junction Railway now form the backbone of the central section of the West Coast Main Line. This book provides the reader with an opportunity to re-trace Osborne's 1838 journey during the year of the Queen Victoria's Coronation. Wildfire through Staffordshire is not only a must have for all railway enthusiasts, but will have an appeal to everybody that is interested in our country's history and heritage.

David Moore M.A. Public History

LIST OF PRINCIPAL PLATES – MAPS, TOWN PLANS, VIEWS AND VISTAS

CONTENTS

VIEW ACROSS BIRMINGHAM FROM THE COVENTRY ROAD 1838

A WARM AND WELCOME PEACEFUL NIGHT'S REST – BIRMINGHAM 1838

The smoky outline of the steeples and factory chimneys of Birmingham at last come into view, we would arrive now surely, well before dark, something of a blessing now as our long and weary coach journey was coming to an end. On down the wide open roadway of Deritend High Street, we pass the many – gabled "Old Crown House", on the banks of the River Rea. This house was built, mainly of timber, around the late 14th century, and consisted of a large Central Hall, with small rooms on each side of the ground floor, and a "Great Chamber" and other rooms on the first floor.

This very old Birmingham house has interesting associations. The "Great Chamber" became the "Gallorye Chamber". In it, according to tradition, Queen Elizabeth passed a night. The house was positioned so as to experience and witness much of the history of this town: Prince Rupert during the Civil War in the Battle of Birmingham and the gallant struggle the Birmingham people made to prevent his entering of the town at this point: Of Shakespeare, who may have journeyed past during

THE OLD CROWN INN - DERITEND - BIRMINGHAM

his early days of Warwickshire rambling, through the pretty street as he entered Birmingham?

And what of most recently, I remember the news of the disastrous Birmingham "King and Country" riots of 1791, directed at Joseph Priestly. Several buildings were destroyed and many lost their lives, although only a young man at that time I feared the mob may visit my town at Stratford. Only a half mile from this spot back then, the mob had set fire to Joseph Priestley's dwelling and destroyed his invaluable philosophical library. The Scarcity Riots had followed in 1795. The distress of the country, caused partly by the oppressive war taxation, and partly by the failure of the harvest and consequent scarcity and expense of wheat, drove many of the poorer classes to distraction, and their discontent found rent in numerous outbreaks against the millers and farmers, and the wealthier classes of the country. Rioting broke out in Birmingham in the June of 1795, and led to serious and fatal results.

After the passing of the Reform Bill in 1832, for which the Birmingham people and those in the nearby Mining and Manufacturing districts had been instrumental, there has been a political lull in England for a few years. The middle classes, being satisfied with the success they had achieved for themselves, had not troubled themselves very much for the extension of the franchise to the working classes. So long as trade remained, and wages were easily earned, the masses would remain quiet. However the disastrous panics of last year has altered this state of affairs: trade was now depressed, bad harvests and the new Corn Laws has driven up the price of bread, wages are falling, work is now becoming scarce and manufacturing in many places had entirely closed.

Early this year, half a dozen Members of Parliament united with a like-size group of working men to compose "The People's Charter" with six main demands for the working classes: universal suffrage, vote by ballot, equal electoral districts, annual Parliaments, abolition of the property qualification for MP's, and payment of Members. In Birmingham, meetings were now being held every Monday evening at the open space around Holloway Head. Only last month there had been a huge demonstration with a reputed 100,000 people gathered to hear the voices of their speakers. During our coach journey fellow travellers spoke of the "uneasy atmosphere" in Birmingham, I just wished for a peaceful night in Birmingham before my intrepid journey the next morning – up along the Grand Junction Railway, the first journey on board "a locomotive", maybe this new phenomena will contribute to prosperity, growth and a nation at peace without war, we can but pray.

We now proceed along what may be the only really picturesque street in Birmingham, Digbeth Street, the White Hart Inn stands to our right, then also on the right, the George Inn. We now pass up through Birmingham "Bull Ring", in this great triangle of space with the magnificent St Martin's church as its base, gather all the outdoor traders of Birmingham. Considerable alterations have been made to St. Martin's. The church dates back to the 13th century, and back in 1781, the spire was found to be in a decayed and exceedingly unsafe condition, and had to be replaced and rebuilt. Alterations also took place inside the church, which included new pews. We now see the distinctive statue of Lord Nelson at the centre, the first to be put up in Britain back in 1809, and then to our left, the grand Market Hall only recently erected, now overlooking the barrow boys and dealers.

As soon as we pass the New Market Hall, the

THE BULL RING BIRMINGHAM AND ST MARTIN'S CHURCH

Charlotte Street

St Paul's Chapel

Jenkens & Bettridges

Scotch Church

Constitution Hill

Birmingham & Fazeley Canal

Maryann St. Henrietta St.

Water Street

Summer L.

General Hospital

LIONEL STREET

Iudgate Street

GREAT CHARLES STREET

Shadwell Street

Steelhouse L.

Roman Catholic Chapel

Edmund Street

Bread Street

Little Charles St.

Meeting House

To the Botanical Gardens

Town Hall

SNOW HILL

St Mary's Chapel

Christ Church

Ann Street

Infant School

Colmore Row

Collis & Co.

New St Hotel

Society of Arts

Post Office

Waterloo Street

News Room

Library Room

St Phillips Church

ROW

Monmouth Street

Blue Coat School

Rollasons

Theatre

Temple Street

Rectory

Steelhouse Lane

Newton St.

National School

Royal Hotel

Square

Work House

Lichfield Street

Peck Lane

Union Street

New Street

Fire Office

Stock Hotel

Grammar School

DALE END

Hen & Chickens Hotel

Albion Hotel

St Peters Church

Moor Street

Worcester Street

Swan Hotel

High Street

Castle Hotel

Proposed

NEW STREET

Chapel St.

St Bartholomew's Chapel

Nelson Hotel

Nelson Statue

Public Office

Digbeth St.

Bull Ring

St Martin's Church

Jamaica Row

George Inn

White Hart Inn

Edgbaston Street

Park Street

Bordesley Street

RAILWAY STATIONS

Goods Depot

Smithfield Market

Allison Street

Meriden Street

Booking Office

Engine House

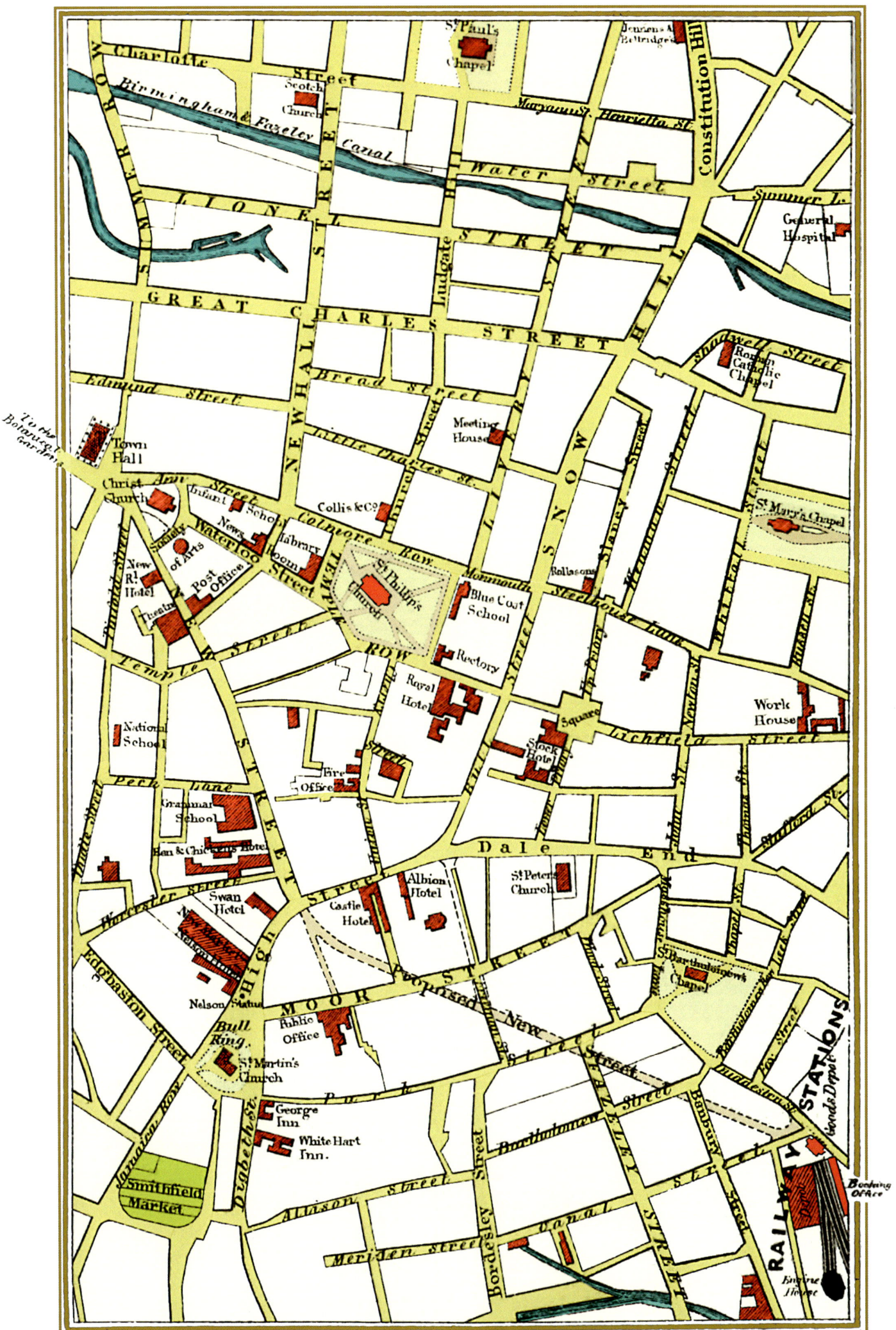

STREET PLAN OF CENTRAL BIRMINGHAM 1838

SWANN HOTEL - HIGH STREET - BIRMINGHAM

coachman steers sharply in to our left into the welcoming entrance yard of the Swann Hotel. Our baggage soon unloaded, a welcome meal, the finest ale, and then a night of quiet contemplation ensues. Despite the need for sleep and aching bones, my thoughts turn to the eagerly awaited journey up along the Grand Junction Railway, across the entire county of Staffordshire, into Cheshire, then Lancashire and on to Liverpool. Yet how safe are these locomotives, people were inclined to believe in the new engines which could travel twice as fast as stage coaches, but also imagined all sorts of difficulties. In rural districts they were afraid that the smoke of the iron horse may harm the fleeces of the sheep or that of an occasional straying cow would prove a catastrophic obstacle for the train. Others feared that the sparks from the engine may set fire to adjoining properties along the line. Despite opposition from many parties, two great railway works had now been opened, connecting the three large manufacturing towns of Birmingham, Manchester and Liverpool with the metropolis,

the Grand Junction Railway in 1837, and this year, the London to Birmingham Railway.

Last year the Birmingham Journal gave a splendid account of the opening train leaving Birmingham, bound for Liverpool and Manchester. "At 7 o clock precisely in the morning, the bell rang, when the opening train, drawn by the "Wildfire" engine, commenced moving. The train consisted of eight carriages, all of the first class, and bearing the following names: Greyhound, Swallow, Liverpool and Birmingham Mail, Celerity, Umpire, Statesman, and Birmingham and Manchester Mail! The train started slowly; but emerging from the yard at the temporary station at Vauxhall, speedily burst off at a rapid rate. To those who for the first time witnessed such a scene it was peculiarly exciting, and the immense multitude, as far as the eye could reach, gave expression to their admiration by loud and long-continued huzzas, and the waving of hats and hankerchiefs".

The morning in Birmingham was to be brief, just enough time to take a quick tour round the centre before making our way to Curzon Street and the Birmingham station of the Grand Junction railway. The recent plan of Birmingham shows the intended, much needed new road connecting the centre, as currently we will need to weave our way through several streets to get to Curzon Street. Before that let us take a short trip around the centre and view some more buildings of note.

Turning to our left and then up along New Street, the first building we pass is the Hen and Chickens Hotel, however adjacent is the newly opened magnificent King Edward's School built by Sir Charles Barry. This is the third building on the site; the school having been founded by King Edward VI in 1552. The original plan by Sir Charles Barry also incorporated a spire on the roof, however the school cost far more to build than the original estimate and the spire was not included, yet however it is undoubtedly a beautiful building. We turn left into Peck Lane, known as the "Froggary" district, a network of crowded courts and alleys, and come to the Birmingham

KING EDWARD'S SCHOOL NEXT TO THE HEN AND CHICKENS HOTEL - NEW STREET BIRMINGHAM

HILL STREET UP TO BIRMINGHAM TOWN HALL

National School, established in 1812, on the corner of Peck Lane. We work our way around the streets and start to climb Hill Street, a large temple shaped building immediately dominates the skyline at the summit. Designed and built by the young partnership of J. A. Hansom and E. Welch, the imposing Birmingham Town Hall is a building from the end of the Classical Revival and a close copy of the Temple of Castor & Pollux in the Forum of Rome, standing on large rough cut stones; it is built of brick, faced with Anglesey stone, with forty feet high Corinthian columns. The basement forms a promenade that offers standing room for over 1,500 people. The main part of the interior consists of one large hall – the object of the building being the accommodation of public meetings and other large assemblies, with a capacity for about 4000 people sitting, but more than double that when standing up.

As we start to proceed back down from the top end of New Street we can see Christ Church, built in 1805 by public subscription to alleviate the shortage of free seats in the town. To our left are the Society of Arts and just a little further down on the right the Theatre. At this point we now turn left up Bennett's Hill with the Post office on the

CHRIST CHURCH

BANK OF BIRMINGHAM - BENNETT'S HILL

ST PHILIP'S CHURCH

corner. This street being a mixture of elegant town houses, banks and commercial premises was only constructed about 15 years ago and now forms the legal and insurance centre of the town and now considered the premier street architecturally. We now pass over Waterloo Street with the News Rooms on our left and turn right into Colmore Row. Here we admire the church of St Philips on our right built by Thomas Archer, picturesquely surrounded by its churchyard and avenues of trees. Thomas Archer was the only English architect of the generation after Wren who knew Italian Baroque at first hand. It is the Borromi like treatment of details such as pediments, and the use of dramatically contrasting convex and concave shapes which make the building of St. Philips so remarkable. The bells chime out as we pass along Colmore Row; the musical interlude summons us to our scheduled destination of departure from Birmingham.

We hastily now make our way past the Blue Coat School on our right, founded as a charity school under the guidance of Reverend William Higgs, Rector of St Philip's Church back in 1722, along Monmouth Street and turn right into Bull Street. Bull Street is the principal street in Birmingham and for retail business and contains some very excellent shops. At the bottom of Bull Street we turn left into Dale End and pass another church, St Peter's, on our right. We turn right down Masshouse Lane passing St Bartholomew's Chapel, into Duddeston Street noting that the streets are now seemingly busy with people and carriages; we enter into Curzon Street with little time to spare.

THE BIRMINGHAM STATION OF THE GRAND JUNCTION RAILWAY

The Birmingham Station of the Grand Junction Railway is situated on a somewhat triangular site, at the front of which is Curzon Street. It is composed of an extensive frontage, with large gates, an interior yard, convenient booking offices, and spacious and elegant shedding. The buildings are erected on the new-red-sandstone formation, which has been extensively excavated in the neighbourhood, the whole side of an opposite hill having been removed, so that high sand cliffs have been formed in the immediate proximity, on which a great portion of the station has been built. A branch of the Birmingham and Warwick Canal is adjacent to the back part of the station.

Close by its site there is the splendid Station of the London and Birmingham Railroad, consisting of a massive and magnificent building for the offices, a handsome line of booking offices, two beautiful and gigantic sheds, from under which the trains start, and at which they arrive, and the engine house, a circular building with a prodigiously strong floor for the reception of the engines.

To a stranger coming into the station-yard for the first time, the whole scene is one of great novelty: the long train of treble-bodied coaches, waiting under a broad covered way for passengers and baggage; the bustle and animation of the host of porters, guards, and conductors.

On entering the yard we find, amidst the greater apparent confusion, the most perfect order. A porter is ready to conduct us to the booking office, where were we pay our fares and receive our tickets. If you travel by a first class ticket, as we are privileged to do so, your ticket will be numbered, corresponding to the number of the seat you will occupy. The second class tickets are not numbered; in this case your ticket will admit you to any seat.

Now may be a good time to inform you of one of the company regulations that is strictly enforced. You cannot offer any gratuities to any of its servants. The consequence is, that instead of that unpleasant and selfish obsequiousness, and that disposition to insult, which persons of this class usually practice, the greatest civility is experienced, questions are replied to in a respectful manner, and when you have received all the attention which you require, without any request on the part of the porter to be "remembered" either by a touch of the hat, or by an insolent scowl, he walks away quickly to attend to the next person who may happen to arrive.

After we have paid our fare and received our ticket we can pass on to the parapet, a porter immediately takes our luggage and places it all on the top of the carriage in which we are going to travel. Exactly at five minutes before our time of departure a bell rings it note of preparation, and we can now step from the parapet into one of the luxuriant and reposing carriages that have been provided for us, bearing the number on the outside and directly over the seat we are expected to occupy corresponding to our ticket number. The first class carriages are divided into three compartments, each containing six places, making eighteen seats in each carriage. These are fitted up in the most costly style; cushioned throughout, and affording plenty of room. The second class carriages have no such compartments, and though not affording the same comfort as the first class, still they greatly surpass the outside of any coach, and are cheaper notwithstanding. We will soon find ourselves travelling along with a sumptuous train, led by the Wildfire.

The scenes at this place, immediately before the starting of the train, is irresistibly striking, and greatly resembles the bustle and variety which give

CURZON STREET STATION

so much animation to the piers and promenades of the fashionable watering places on the coast.

Looking out from the carriage we see several engines with red hot fires in their bodies, and volumes of steam issuing from their tall chimneys. One of them cautiously moves slowly towards you. The huge creature bellows, at first like an elephant. Deep, slow, and terrific are the hoarse heavings that it makes. It passes by your train of carriages, and going to the head of them, slips from one line to the other, and backing up to the train of carriages, is fastened to it. There it stands, roaring, groaning, and grunting, like a sea horse, and spouting up steam like a whale. You feel a deep, strong, tremulous motion throughout the train, and an almost deafening jingling rattle reverberates all around.

As we pursue our course we will cast our eyes to the right and to the left upon the interesting objects of our flying route, which will seem to move past us like so many novel and beautiful scenes of an ever shifting panorama. Indeed as we begin our journey we may ponder about time itself, time which is the great desideratum or loss in journeys, that it will be a very small item in the amount of travelling. Beautiful indeed that we may at some stage in the development of the railways go from Birmingham to Liverpool or Manchester in an hour and half. That London and Liverpool are brought so close together, as they will be, that we may breakfast in one place, and dine at the other, we shall have the Manchester merchant attending the London Stock Exchange, and returning home to tea.

CURZON STREET STATION

APPROACHING ASTON CHURCH AND VIADUCT AT THE START OF THE JOURNEY 1838

THE JOURNEY

The conductor takes his seat, the guard is in his box at the back of the carriage and a bell is rung to signal the start. The sound of the engine rushing and plunging reverberates all around as the pace gradually quickens, reaching a speed that far outstrips the fastest mail coach. The rattle of the engine settles down to resemble the clatter of a flour mill. At first it is possible to keep track of the stroke of the piston, but this soon outstrips the count. During the journey many of the miles will be performed in less than a minute.

There can be no better way to appreciate the magnificent and ever-changing scenery than from the carriages of the Wildfire Locomotive. The journey begins in the sprawling industrial town of Birmingham and crosses the Warwickshire border within minutes, heading up through the manufacturing townships of Staffordshire and into Cheshire along the recently opened Grand Junction Railway, connecting with the Liverpool and Manchester Railway to complete the journey.

The country around opens up rapidly and beautifully, each scene then shifting away as if by magic. The locomotive engine seems to be some extraordinary animal with strength of the elephant and the swiftness of the eagle, impelling itself forward at a prodigious rate while it hurls the world away behind it. Despite this, there is the feeling of perfect safety and the rapidity of the motion is a delightful sensation.

The train glides over the canal joining the Birmingham and Fazeley Canal. Both the Birmingham to London and Grand Junction Railway lines pass over this canal on one long, solid, and remarkably strong arch before proceeding along the side of the London line, which – curiously - enters the town parallel to the Grand Junction Liverpool line. In a few yards the line turns off to the right by a noble ten arch viaduct, terminating in a magnificent line of embankment. We enter a large curve nearly a mile in length, the greater part of which is a viaduct of great strength and considerable beauty passing over the valley, through which flows the River Rea.

This viaduct consists of 28 arches, each 31 feet wide and 28 feet above street level. From here there is a fine view of the London and Grand Junction Stations, the London line, and a large part of Birmingham, particularly the Vauxhall side, including Vauxhall Gardens - the principal, if not the only, place of public recreation in the neighbourhood of Birmingham. When I consider that there is no adequate public place of resort for the mass of artisans and inhabitants of Birmingham, we can only hope that the same spirit of improvement and progress of civilization which has given us the railroad, will also, sooner or later, give us a park or public walk, suitable to the needs of Birmingham's inhabitants. This part of the railroad is chiefly remarkable, however, for its curve. It was thought at one time that trains would not move on a curve, the force of the engine only operating in a straight line. It is now clear, however, that a curve - even one as great as this - can be travelled without loss of speed due to an elevation of the outer rail.

Just one and a half miles into our journey

we come to our first Station. Vauxhall Station is exclusively for the reception and forwarding of merchandise of every description and consists of a spacious engine house for the conservation, repair and preparation of the engines; a spacious shed for departing and arriving trains; offices for booking and other business; and sheds for receiving heavy goods.

After passing through a cutting of alluvial gravel 30 feet deep, we pass Duddeston Hall on the right. This place is now a lunatic asylum, being formerly the residence of Samuel Galton. Also on the right is the Village of Saltley, down in the valley. Compared with the large churches of towns, or the magnificent and sublime cathedrals of our cities, the little chapel appears as a miniature pocket church, and you have the feeling that it might be put upon one of the trucks of the train to be carried along for the benefit of travellers. We shortly come to an embankment of 40 feet, from which we can see the neat buildings of Gravelly Hill, in the Parish of Erdington, a village still further to the right. The tall chimney of the Birmingham Water Works, the reservoir of which is observed a little further on, is also seen across to the right. From here the town of Birmingham is supplied with water by means of two magnificent engines of 100 horse power each, which not only force the water to the extremities of the town, but to a large reservoir five miles distant, and 250 feet above the level at which they stand.

The line crosses the Fazeley Canal and Lichfield Road by a 10 arch viaduct, and then proceeds for some distance in the form of a crescent as Aston Church and Hall come into view on the left. These objects are extremely beautiful and deserve more notice than we can devote to them. The church appears situated in the midst of lofty trees, which heighten its scenic beauty, and form a graceful drapery to the chaste and tapering spire above them. The churchyard is one of the most exquisitely rural in the land. A group of estate workers take a break from their labours wave their arms, marvelling at our train as it trundles on its journey, carelessly breaking the early morning silence. This is the most favourable position for obtaining a view of arriving or departing trains as the curved line which the railroad takes keeps the engine and its carriages in view for longer, also giving a variety of views.

Aston Hall is a large stately building of the Elizabethan style of architecture consisting of a

VAUXHALL STATION

The Journey
(Wildfire Locomotive)

We journey on the Grand Junction Railway,
All on board the Wildfire Locomotive;
Faster than a mail coach, its emotive,
The River Tame reflecting the sun`s ray.
Watching farmers turning grass into hay,
A magnificent changing scenery;
Birmingham surrounded by greenery,
An Arcadia on a summer`s day.

The conductor is safely in his seat,
The guard is at the back of the carriage;
We glide along the rails with our baggage
And our new-found happiness is complete.
We wave to everybody we meet,
The engine clattering like a flour mill,
Swifter than a hawk plunging for the kill:
An experience that cannot be beat.

Onwards the Wildfire! Onwards to Cheshire!
The engine plunges and reverberates,
Impelled forward at prodigious rate.
Along the embankments are rousing cheers,
The Wildfire journeying through Staffordshire.
Strength of an elephant, speed of a hawk,
We pass meadows where shepherds point and gawk
And with a blink the Wildfire disappears.

massive and dignified centre, two projecting wings, and out-houses on each side. The centre and wings each have a square tower, with each adorned with a dome and ornamented with a spiral roof and vane. The building is seen and approached through a noble avenue of trees, lending the eastern front of the hall a baronial and dignified appearance. It is the property of Keeling Greenway of Warwick. The present resident is James Watt, the son of the late celebrated Watt - the prince of engineers and the improver, almost the inventor, of the steam engine. By his genius and assiduity he, with his partner Matthew Boulton, established an extensive business, principally in the construction of steam engines, at Soho Forge near Handsworth, a village a little further up the line. He died on August 25th 1819, at the age of 83, leaving behind him a large fortune. It is ponderous to note that the son of the great engineer, James Watt Junior, the now proprietor of Aston Hall, spent £2000 in opposing and preventing the line actually passing through Aston Park, leading to the curved line out of Birmingham described.

The present structure of Aston Church is probably not more than 300 years old, bearing marks of having been erected in the fifteenth century. It is a chaste and beautiful building, having a handsome tower and lofty spire, and is dedicated to Saints Peter and Paul. It appears to be remarkably well preserved; indeed great care has been taken of it and it is adorned with many pieces of ancient sculpture. This church is a favourite resort for those entering into the state of marriage, and it is as creditable to their taste as it is to their feelings when the most important step of life is about to be taken. The church yard might well be designated the Lover's Haunt.

The course of the River Tame, which flows here, has been altered to run on the right or eastern – instead of the western – side of the line. Near to Aston Church are the Aston Tavern and Tea Gardens, which attract a great deal of business in fine weather from the pleasantness of the situation and the taste displayed in the design of the grounds. The line takes a course around Aston Park meaning that the Hall and Church remain in view for nearly two miles, but not withstanding this, the speed at which the train travels renders the view to the passenger but brief after all.

We now cross the boundary of Warwickshire and

ASTON HALL

ASTON HALL AND THE WILDFIRE

Sonnet to Aston Hall

Across a viaduct snakes the Wildfire
To the beautiful Aston Park and Hall,
Home of James Watt and scene of summer balls.
Through the concealing trees pokes a church spire,
Wildfire`s wheels sing like a metallic lyre:
Praise for the Hall, in Jacobean style.
A Garden of Eden, spread over miles,
Birmingham`s country mansion to inspire.

Fishponds and a chestnut-lined avenue,
300 acres and home to fruit trees,
The church set in a graceful drapery.
A Birmingham paradise, seen by few,
Only the lofty church spire is in view.
Aston Hall is domed and flanked by towers,
Perfumed walks beneath, scented bowers,
Standing proud under skies of powdered blue.

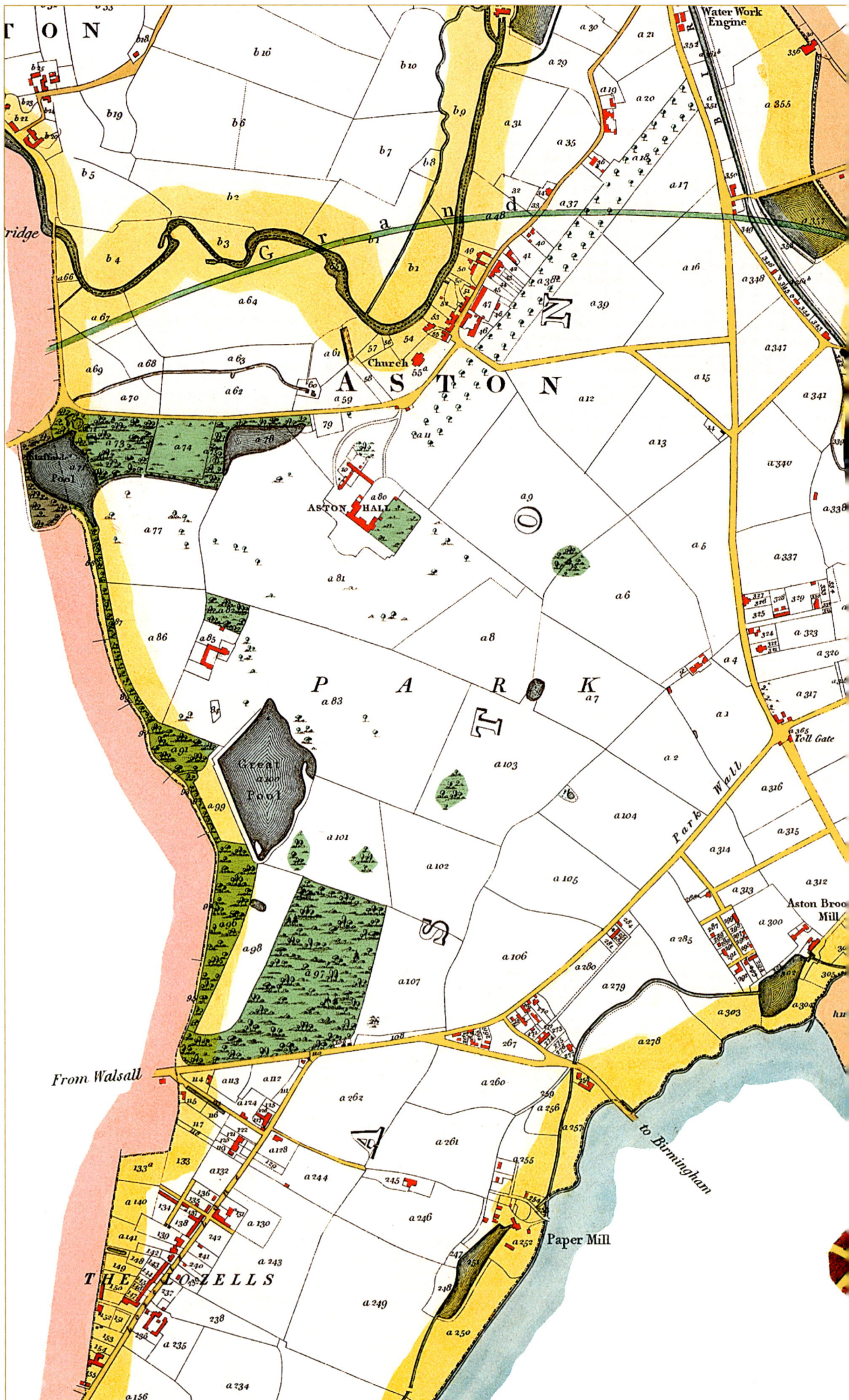

MAP SHOWING PART OF THE PARISH OF ASTON AND NORTH BIRMINGHAM 1833

SALTLEY

Saltley Hall

Thimble
Mill

Chapel

Duddeston
House

Mill

VAUXHALL

Northumberland Place

BARRACKS

Gosta
Green

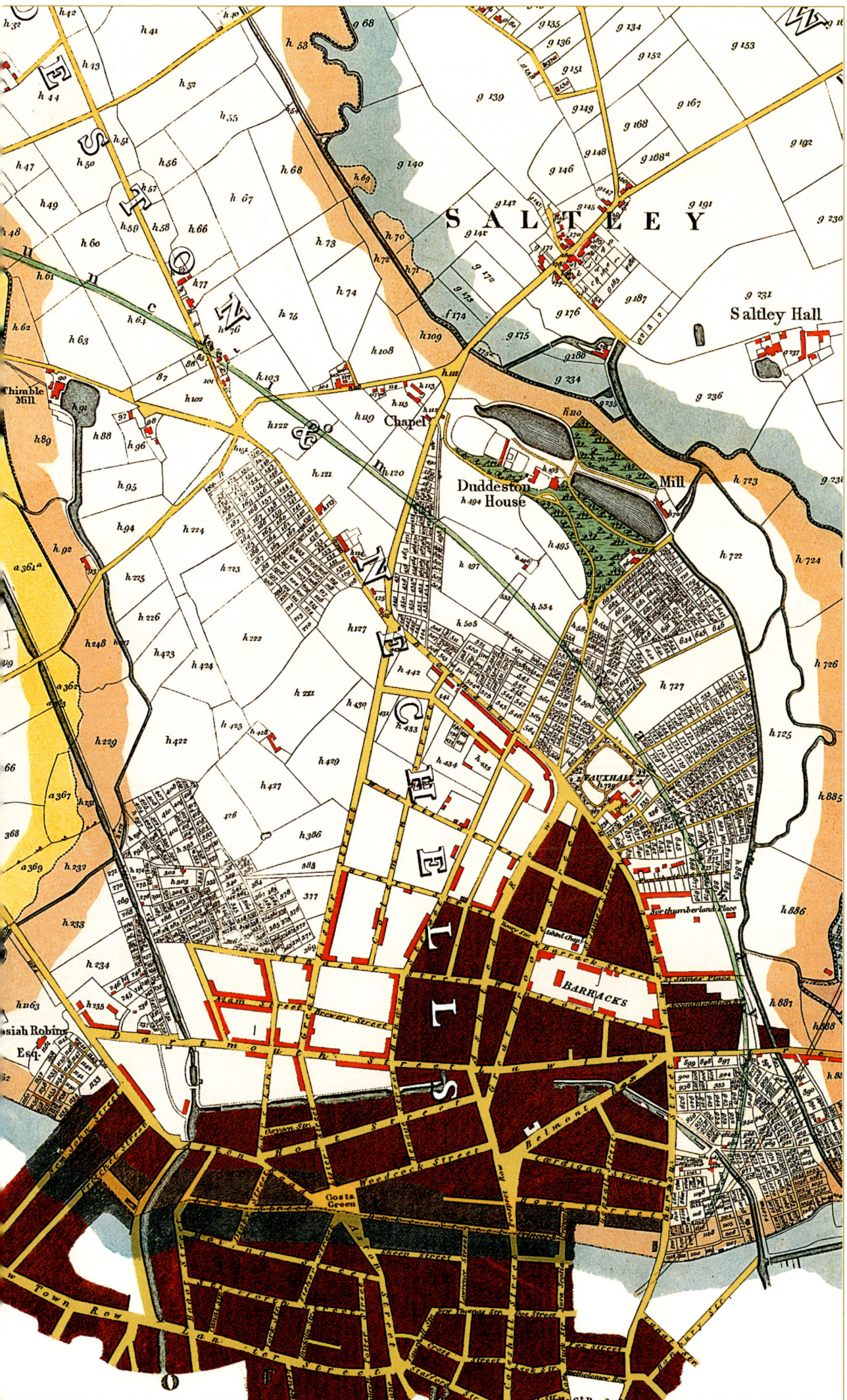

THE PLANNED ROUTE OF THE GRAND JUNCTION RAILWAY IS SHOWN IN GREEN

SOHO MANUFACTORY FROM THE NINEVEH ROAD 1838

Tomb of James Watt, St Mary`s Church, Handsworth (acrostic)

James Watt - inventor, prince of engineers
And patents for industry he designed;
Matthew Boulton and he were pioneers,
Experiments with their brilliant minds.
Steam engines from their Soho factory

World dominance of manufacturing;
An important person in history,
This Handsworth resident had top ranking,
The godfather of British industry.

enter Staffordshire. A part of the village of Erdington may be seen on the right, and at some distance Witton Hall, along with Oldford, the residence of John Willmore, a gentleman of great taste and achievements in botany and entomology, and who possesses one of the finest private collections of entomological specimens in the kingdom. On the hill to the right stands the New Catholic College of Oscott, a large, well built, and conveniently arranged structure used to educating youths and young men for priesthood or for public life.

We then pass through a cutting of fine alluvium on red sandstone and soon arrive at the first of the second class stations, Perry Barr Station. Here we pass under an arch, over which is the Birmingham and Walsall Road. On the right is Perry Hall,

enclosed and hidden from view by surrounding stately and ancient trees, and near it stands Perry Church, and elegant, little building, built by John Gough, the proprietor of the hall.

About a mile to the west is the Church of Handsworth, its parish containing many pretty residences, which are chiefly occupied by persons engaged in business at Birmingham. The rectory in the deanery of Tamworth is in the gift of the Right Hon. Sir Robert Peel. The church is nearly as sequestered and interesting as Aston's. It is a handsome Gothic structure of red sandstone, standing in a neat rural yard. The interior is exceedingly elegant and well arranged, but the great attraction is the statue of the late James Watt. This fine work consists of a handsome grey marble pedestal on which, in a

HANDSWORTH CHURCH

PERRY HALL

sitting posture and presented in the act of drawing, is a figure of Watt carved in pure white marble. The figure seems alive and is one of the most successful efforts of Chantrey, one of the greatest of all British sculptors. The statue was commissioned to honour Watt's memory, and his son, the present occupier of Aston Hall, built a small chapel for its reception on the north side of the church, to the right of the altar. In this piece of sculpture, Watt and Chantrey are immortalized together. To the left of the altar is a bust of Boulton, Watt's partner.

On leaving Perry Barr we pass through a cutting of alluvial gravel more than 20 feet deep, and to the left, on a hill, is a handsome brick house, the residence of Mrs Mary Boddington. Perry Hall and the previously-seen wood are seen on the right for some time, and the scenery is altogether very beautiful. We then pass over an iron bridge of three arches which spans the Tame. This beautiful little river crosses the road several times, and winds through the valley for a considerable distance, giving rise to enchanting scenery, which makes one desire to remain in the area longer.

We pass under a bridge over which lies the Old Walsall road and, leaving a mill with a pretty stream which turns it on the right, we enter an almost 60 feet deep cutting through a place called Pixton's Hill, named after the works contractor for part of the line. The strata consist of alluvial gravel about eighteen feet thick, beneath which is the newer, red sandstone, with intervening layers of marl. We then arrive at a rich and luxuriant valley, called Hampstead. On the hill to the left is Hampstead Hall, the residence of T. L. Moilliett, a Birmingham banker. This place is beautifully situated in the midst of a wood on the banks of the Tame, with meadows lying between it and the road. On both sides of the line the luxuriance of the surrounding countryside is both delightful and exhilarating.

About a mile to the south-west, and behind Hampstead Hall, are Sandwell Park and Hall, the residence of The Right Hon Earl of Dartmouth. The hall stands on a splendid sloping lawn, adorned with old trees and skirted by woods. A large lake beautifies the north side, and along the water's course lie a number of little islands constructed by the owner. The hall is a plain and substantial modern building, square and low, having a south front entrance with the rising park before it, with the east and north front looking out on the park's descent. It is said to have taken its name from Santa Fons, a Holy Well, but we do not know why one

The Sand Well (acrostic)

This little well founded a priory
Hewn from sandstone and near the River Tame,
Earnestly pouring out into the valley

Sandwell - it gave this area its name.
A life-giver, its sadly overlooked
Now clean and fresh water comes out of taps.
Dumbed down in history, left out of books,

Water, the source of life on ancient maps.
Enduring centuries, water still flows,
Laughter bubbling from rocks as it goes,
Light as a feather and sweet as a rose

portion of the old Latin name is preserved and the remainder translated into English. What is certain, however, is that in front of the hall, in the ascent of the park, there is a well named the Holy Well.

The site of the hall was occupied earlier by the Benedictine Monks who founded a Priory. During the Reformation, when religious houses were put down, it was given to Thomas Lord Cromwell, from whom it has passed to its present possessor. The estate is very valuable from both the nature of the land and the coal and iron mines it contains. The mansion contains some very valuable paintings by the first masters, but as his lordship does not like his house to be shown, few know anything about them. This nobleman is well known in his neighbourhood as an active Conservative, a liberal

SANDWELL HALL AND PARK

NEWTON ROAD STATION.

contributor to, and patron of, every charitable and scientific institution. His benevolence to the poor of the neighbourhood makes him justly and deservedly appreciated.

The tall chimneys of Messrs Chance Brothers & Co's Crown Glass Works and Messrs Adkins & Co's Soap Works at Smethwick appear in the distance among the trees to the west. We then pass a deep cutting of 80 feet through Newton Hill, a bed of clayey marl, and arrive at Newton Road Station. We pass under the bridge that supports the road to West Bromwich and Barr and find ourselves surrounded by verdant meadows with the River Tame to one side. On the hill to the west is Charley Mount, the residence of Joseph Aldford Esq, in the parish of West Bromwich.

Our train enters a steady bend and we now see the town of Wednesbury about a mile and a half to the west of the line, and two miles further north of the town of West Bromwich. It was, very early in the history of our country, a place of importance, its name derived from Woden, the Saxon God of War, and Boro or Burgo, the name of a town. A strong fortress was erected on the hill where the Church now stands by Ethelfleda, daughter of Alfred the Great, in 916. The place stands on a hill and is surrounded by tall chimneys, engine houses, and machinery of coal pits, furnaces and iron works.

Wednesbury is a dark, dirty looking town, as though cleanliness and comfort were none of its care. The population is now 9000 or more. The Church is a handsome Gothic building, lately repaired at large expense. The living is a discharged vicarage in the archdeaconry of Stafford and diocese of Lichfield and Coventry. There are three chapels, one belonging to the Independents, one to the Methodists, and one to the Primitive Methodists. This is one of the places that saw furious mobs when first the Wesleyans began their outdoor preaching.

There is a Lancastrian School - built by subscription - educating 130 boys, a Church Sunday School, and a Methodist School. William, the first Lord Paget and Secretary of State to Henry VIII, was once a native of this town.

MINE WORKINGS AT WEDNESBURY

The mines of coal, iron and lime, and the manufacture of gun-locks and barrels, axle-trees, and springs for coaches, hinges, nails, screws, files, gas and water tubing, afford the population tolerable full employment. The surrounding country seems turned inside-out; worked in all directions for ironstone, coal and limestone, the pits varying in depth from 60 to 230 yards.

On the 9th of December 1824, a large steam engine boiler at the gun-iron factory of Mr Richard Adams suddenly burst with terrific force. The explosion was so tremendous that nearly all the engine machinery was damaged, and the walls and roof of the engine-house – which included two lofty stacks of chimneys - were reduced to heaps of rubble, with debris thrown a considerable distance in various directions. The accident saw the dreadful loss of the lives of Mr Adams and four of his workmen, one of whom was found at a distance of 120 yards from the works. The boiler was 20 feet long and 20 feet high, and was supposed to have exploded due to the safety valve becoming over-weighted.

There is a market every Friday and cattle fairs are held on the 6th May and the 3rd of August. There is also a wake, or feast, that begins on the Sunday before Bartholomew's day, at which times the most fearful displays of intemperance are witnessed. During the war, most of the men could have become independent, so high were their wages and so constant their employment, yet few of them are now possessed of even basic necessities. The

The 1824 Steam Engine Explosion in Wednesbury

Railway cuts through the land for noisy trains,
Carriage witnesses to this hinterland,
A grim world that I cannot understand.
Chimneys belch downpours of soot and black rain,
Factories hammering out heavy chains,
A beat from its manufacturing heart.
Whilst blast furnaces blow the sky apart,
Coal miners head down to the pits again.

I record the present for the future,
Human lives pass but their stories remain;
Lit, like colours, in stained glass window panes.
As I witness the Staffordshire culture,
Scene of Industrial Revolution ,
Soot from forges causes air pollution,
A manufacturing heart to nurture.

So it was that only through God's great grace
No huge loss of life when an engine burst.
A mighty explosion, as if God cursed,
The engine machinery was displaced.
A tremendous sound that was heard in space
The owner and four workmen sadly died
And sad tears the widows and orphans cried,
Their loved ones that nobody could replace.

Standing silent in mourning, winding gears
Overlooking Wednesbury and coal mines.
The Wildfire journey on railway lines,
The present recorded and yesteryear.
Steam engine explosion, sad lonely tears
And carried away down the mineshaft holes
Like God, on Judgement Day, will harvest souls
As Wildfire picks up speed and disappears.

principal inns of the town are the Dartmouth Arms, the Green Dragon, the Turk's Head, the Red Lion, and the Talbot.

Looking out across the meadows, the high hill in the distance is dominated by the town of Walsall. It is an ancient borough and has lately become a growing market town. It lies about a mile and a half to the east of the line of the rail road. On the loftiest part of the hill the parish church commands a grand view. Walsall now contains about 20,000 inhabitants and encompasses "the foreign of Walsall" and "the Chapelry of Bloxwich." The Earl of Bradford is Lord of the Manor.

The parish church, a handsome and modern Gothic cruciform structure, with a tower and lofty spire, is situated at the top of the hill in the centre of the town. With the exception of the tower and chancel - which have undergone several alterations - it was taken down in 1821 and rebuilt in the later style of English architecture, based on a design by Mr Godwin. The living is a vicarage and is in the gift of the Right Hon. Earl of Bradford. In the south part of the town, near the church, there is a new burial ground, and close to it is the Vicarage house, shaded by trees.

Down on the left side hand of Bridge Street, enclosed in a small burial ground, is St. Paul's Chapel. A small Grecian structure, it serves as a chapel-of-ease and was built by the governors of the Grammar School in 1826. In addition to St. Paul's chapel there is a Methodist, Baptist, Independent, Unitarian, and two Roman Catholic chapels, one of which displays a handsome edifice, in the Grecian style of architecture.

There is a Free Grammar School in Park Street which was founded by Queen Mary in 1557 and endowed with 298 acres of land, which brings in an annual rent. The school and its funds are placed in the hands of ten trustees. Bishop Hough, a great champion of religious liberty who was committed to the Tower by James II, received the rudiments of his education at this school. The governors have built an English school for 120 boys, a school for boys at Walsall Wood, and two infant schools.

In St. Paul's place there is a Blue Coat School,

housed in a handsome building, the institution principally supported by private subscription. There is a National School at Walsall Wood, which educates 300 boys and 300 girls, of whom 25 of each sex are clothed by charity. There is a large room here let for public lectures, concerts, and other functions.Every place of worship has its own Sunday school, and some of them have day schools attached to them.

Mollesleys's Alms Houses in Dudley-street contain 11 dwellings for poor women who receive two shillings each per week. During the reign of Henry VI, Thomas Mollesley gave the corporation a manor and estates in Warwickshire for the purpose of distributing a dole of 1*d* to every person in the parish on the eve of the Epiphany. In 1825, these alms houses were erected and endowed, to which purpose the dole was appropriated. Hooper's Alms Houses in Dudley Street consist of residences for six poor women and there are many other Charities besides these for clothing and feeding the poor, apprenticing poor boys, and for other useful purposes. A curious custom of throwing apples and nuts from the Town Hall on St Clements day to be scrambled for by the populace continues here. The New Poor Law Union Workhouse is a large building, some little way out of town, and the business of the poor is managed by a Board of Guardians. There is a Savings Bank near the Blue Coat School.

The public buildings are few. The Town Hall is in High Street, where the corporations transact their business. The Library and News room, in Lichfield Street, is a very handsome building with a massive portico supported by Doric pillars. The theatre is a small building of little consequence and the Grand Stand at the Race Course is only thought of by those at the Races. The inns are generally of a very superior order. The principal one is the George Hotel, which is a very handsome building, with a massive front consisting of four large pillars, which were removed from the mansion of Lord Spencer at Fisherwick. The others are the Dragon and Royal Oak, the New Inn, the Turk's Head, the Royal Oak, and the Bradford Arms. There are many handsomely built houses in the suburbs and

Sonnet for St Matthew`s Church Bells
(Walsall Parish Church)

Hear the sound of St Matthew`s church bells ring,
Wildfire riding the Grand Junction Railway.
The church on the hill takes the breath away,
Witness to Walsall`s manufacturing.
The bells, like prayers, call out to Christ the King.
The church is built in cruciform structure,
Seen for miles, its Gothic architecture,
Pews are filled by workers in thanksgiving.

The devotion of Walsall does inspire,
Sustenance in limestone mining and coal pits.
Words of faith delivered from the pulpit
As the bells peal around the lofty spire.
Working conditions down the mines is dire,
Lower classes fill the congregation.
Walsall is saddlery to the nation,
Church bells ring and onwards rolls the Wildfire.

outskirts, and the roads leading to the town are very good, wide and noble looking.

The celebrated Lord Somers was educated in this town and Mr Siddons, the husband of the celebrated Mrs Siddons, the tragic actress, was born here. The borough is governed by the Mayor and 24 council-men and has a recorder, who may hold a Court of Record every week, and sends one member to Parliament under the provisions of the 1832 Reform Act.

The market is on Tuesday, when there is a good supply of most articles of use. Three fairs are held here: on February 24th, on Whit Tuesday – a pleasure fair - and one on Tuesday before old Michaelmas Day, chiefly for horses, cattle, cheese and onions. A wake is held on the Sunday before the fair and the races take place on the Wednesday and Thursday after.

A very beautiful kind of grey limestone is found here, which makes excellent stucco work, being nearly equal to plaster of Paris. It is found in great abundance at the Hayhead mines. The country all around abounds with lime and coal.

The manufacture of the district, as well as the town of Walsall, is that of saddlers' and coach-makers' ironmongery, as well as saddles, bridles, and harnesses. This is the emporium of the world for these things. Buckles, chains, curbs, bits, spurs, and stirrups are made also in great abundance, manufactured by the pound or stone. Great numbers of little smiths make separate articles, or perform one process only of an article; each different part of the material is thus brought to the factors. Men, women, boys and girls may all work at it, and frequently do, but with all their diligence, they are not able to obtain much by their labour, especially of late. It is a light business, requiring but little capital, and therefore great numbers crowd into it, bringing down the profits to a minimum.

Enough materials are manufactured in this neighbourhood during each year to make as many as 20,000 saddles and bridles for equestrian purposes and for 200,000 sets of harness for coaches, carriages, gigs, teams etc. These are sent to all parts of the kingdom, and to almost every part of the world.

The working people are certainly more cultivated here than in most other parts of the mining and manufacturing district, but they are still far

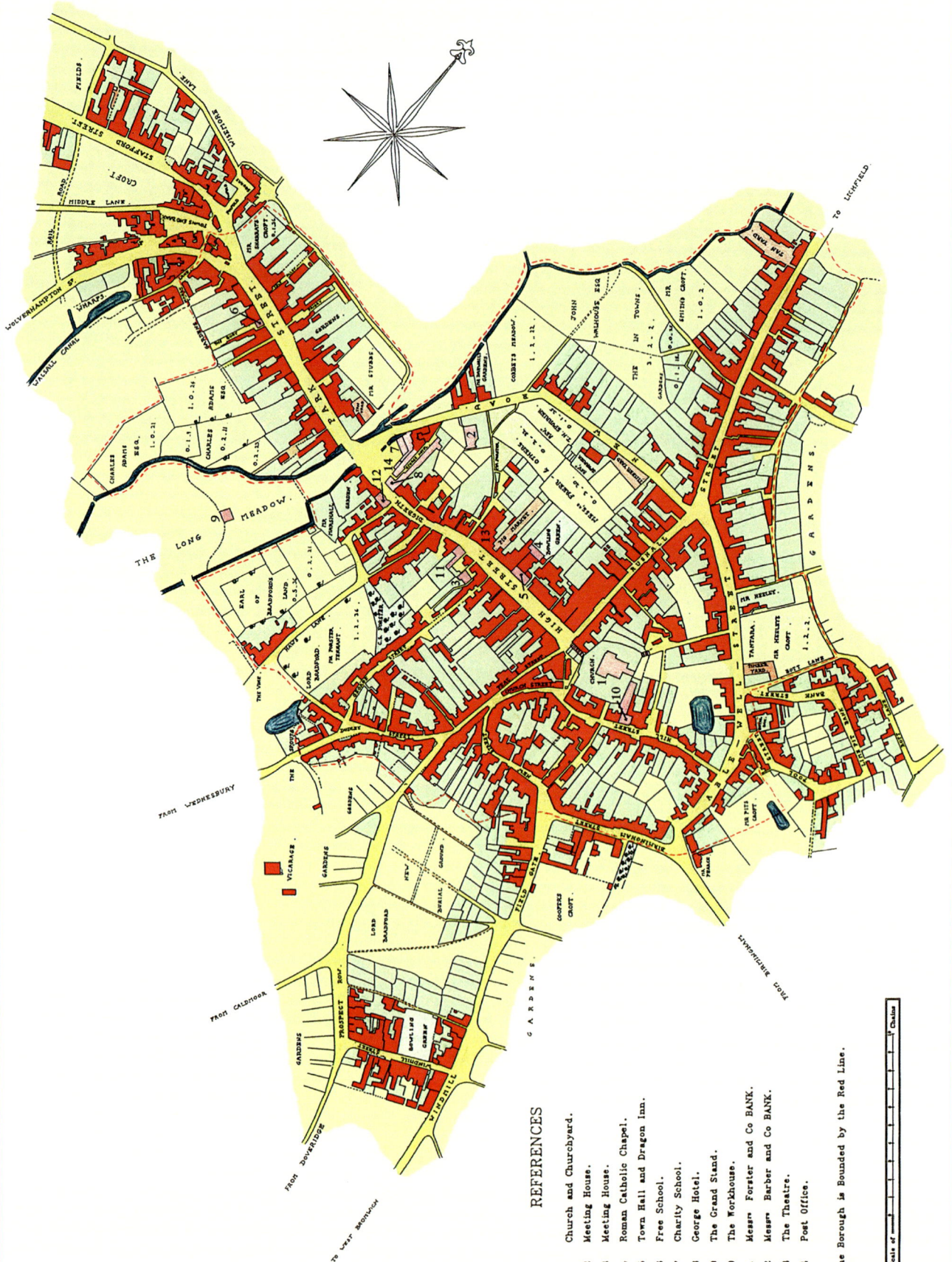

MASON'S PLAN OF WALSALL 1824

REFERENCES

1   Church and Churchyard.
2   Meeting House.
3   Meeting House.
4   Roman Catholic Chapel.
5   Town Hall and Dragon Inn.
6   Free School.
7   Charity School.
8   George Hotel.
9   The Grand Stand.
10   The Workhouse.
11   Messrs Forster and Co BANK.
12   Messrs Barber and Co BANK.
13   The Theatre.
14   Post Office.

The Borough is Bounded by the Red Line.

Scale of Feet
1 Chains

The Mining & Manufacturing District
Seen from the Wildfire Locomotive

A coal seam runs across South Staffordshire
Known to the Romans and 30 feet thick;
Where miners descend, out "into the thick"
And fumes are hurled up into the atmosphere.
Only on the Wrekin is the air clear,
Coal-fired furnaces pumping out flames:
Noxious air, slag heaps, Hell in all but name,
Wildfire just passing through, bound for Cheshire.

The earth pockmarked where industry has been,
A network of canals are the highway
For South Staffordshire in these glory days.
Vegetation succumbed, no fields of green,
Widespread devastation, no shrubs are seen.
An image of Hell across the coal field,
Black diamonds and gold the coal seam does yield,
Not pastoral idylls with waters clean.

Embraced under a darkened canopy,
Hard graft now in an industrial age;
World renown, South Staffordshire`s heritage,
Black as the coal dug from the collieries.
Locks, boiling cauldrons, tubes and foundries,
Geological minerals the backbone:
Iron-making based on coal and limestone,
Development of heavy industry.

Disembowelled earth is seen for miles around
Out of the coal mines the black gold is won,
A constant cloud of smoke blocks out the sun.
The landscape is broken by cinder mounds,
Furnace refuse where iron ore is bound
And then being run out into the pig beds,
The smelting process from the funnel heads
And ore, coal and limestone from underground.

Nothing by day but burning furnaces
And mountains of cinder and earth laid bare;
Manufacturing at night under glare
Of lurid smoke-stacks and dirty faces.
Day and night the same under the surface
For men of iron harvesting the coal
In mine shafts, "in the thick", deep in their holes:
Calloused hands, backs bent and far from God`s Grace.

Air pollution confuses day and night
For those in workshops and down the coal pits;
Dudley`s chains and Walsall`s bridle bits,
Wolverhampton`s locks made by candle light.
Anchors and cables forged by Cradley`s might,
Oldbury`s saucepans, rivets, bolts and nuts;
Wednesbury`s tubes on the banks of the cut,
Staffordshire industrial dreams burn bright.

removed from the elegancies of polished life. There is a strong political and religious feeling amongst the workmen; most of the places of worship are well attended and the present vicar of the parish church, by his popular mode of address in the pulpit, attracts large congregations.

The line from Newton Road proceeds in a straight direction through fine meadow land and passes Wednesbury Forge, the property of Mr Elwell, a large place for the manufacture of edge tools such as axes, adzes, hoes, spades, and chisels. We then pass under the turnpike road from Wednesbury to Walsall, and arrive at Bescot Bridge Station.

From here we go on, with occasionally pleasant scenery retaining the views of the spires of Walsall and Wednesbury on our right and left, leaving Bescot Hall, the residence of Mr Marshall, a banker of Walsall, on the right. We pass under the road from Bilston to Walsall and arrive at James Bridge Station.

We glide under the bridge erected for the line of the Walsall and Wednesbury road, and to the right is the aqueduct of the Darlaston and Walsall branch of the Birmingham Canal. This is a very magnificent work, as high as 120 feet from the level of Bescot Brook at its centre, and over which it is carried by means of a handsome bridge of two lofty arches. A branch aqueduct goes off to the right to Bentley, a part of the estate of the Earl of Lichfield. Over one part of the aqueduct there is a viaduct for the Bentley road, thus passing a canal over the road, and then a road over the canal.

To the west, about a mile from the line, is the town of Darlaston, part of the mining district of Staffordshire. The town is situated on a hill and from a distance looks very well, but as we approach it a wretchedness more apparent than in any other part of the mining district begins to appear. The buildings are almost all small houses for the workmen and their workshops; and the place is as ill-constructed and rough in appearance, as if there were no town within 100 miles. Many of the streets are as unattended as the lanes of a farm-house, the mud and dirt actually obstructing passage. The population is nearly 7000.

There is a plainly built large church, in modern chapel-of-ease style, which was erected by subscription. The living is a rectory in the archdeaconry of Stafford and diocese of Lichfield and Coventry, and is in the gift of the executors of the late celebrated Reverend Simeon of Cambridge. There is a Wesleyan Methodist chapel, an Independent chapel, and a magnificent Primitive Methodist chapel. This last building is one of the largest and best constructed edifices of the kind in the country. There are Sunday Schools connected with each place of worship, and two National Schools, each capable of receiving 200 scholars and which were built and are supported by subscriptions.

The manufacture of the place is gun locks, a branch of business which, during the war, was so profitable that a good workman could earn a pound note per day. Even granting a considerable allowance for the depreciation of paper money, the employment was so profitable that by working only two days a week the men could obtain as much as would supply their wants, also finding them the means of enjoying the only luxury they seemed to know – that of drinking – in which they used to indulge out of loyalty to their own county, and hatred of France.

During the war, the Darlaston gun lock makers used to live in the most luxurious and extravagant manner. Their demand for poultry, fish and meat was such that Darlaston became the most profitable market for these things in the area. Most of the men might have made fortunes in the days of prosperity, but they not only spent what they obtained extravagantly but also refused to work for more than one or two days a week. During this belligerent carnival, the people sunk even lower than before in vice and immorality, and not one particle of what can be denominated personal or household comfort was obtained. Bull-baiting, dog and cock-fighting, and all sorts of low and debased practices became their amusements, while swearing, cursing and vulgar language seemed to grow with their prosperity. At length the war ceased and suddenly the trade fell away. The workman, instead of being able to get a pound a day, could only obtain three

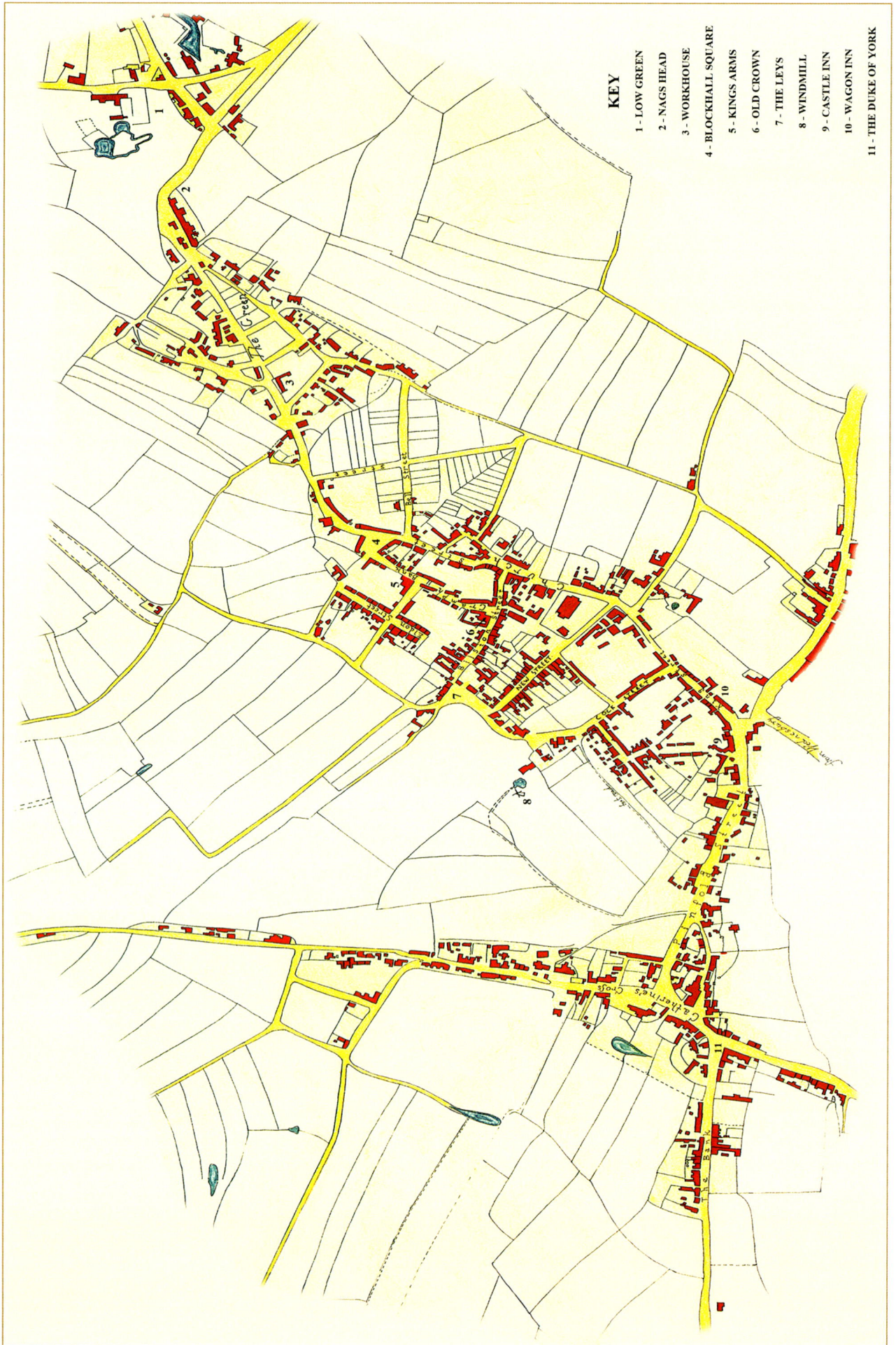

MAP OF THE TOWN OF DARLASTON 1838

KEY

1 - LOW GREEN
2 - NAGS HEAD
3 - WORKHOUSE
4 - BLOCKHALL SQUARE
5 - KINGS ARMS
6 - OLD CROWN
7 - THE LEYS
8 - WINDMILL
9 - CASTLE INN
10 - WAGON INN
11 - THE DUKE OF YORK

The Gun Lock Makers of Darlaston

Darlaston is famous for its gun locks
But the town streets look like farmyard byways;
Its lewd citizens should be put in stocks,
Squalor seen from the Grand Junction Railway.
In the wars, gun lock makers became rich,
Working only a few days in the week:
Two days at work, four spent drunk in a ditch,
Houses in poor repair with roofs that leak.

Bullbaiting, dog and cock fighting, pure sin:
Darlaston loves surrender to drinking,
Swearing, an amusement they indulged in,
Belligerent carnival their thinking.
Low and debased behaviour just uncouth,
Their harsh language is unintelligible
With no proper role models for their youth,
Darlaston people are incorrigible.

Millions of gun locks, their god mammon,
A prosperous town in the neighbourhood.
They dined on plates of chicken and salmon
But in peacetime their wealth was gone for good.
Fortunes made in days of prosperity,
Workmen crafting locks on anvil and forge
Then lost to vice, greed, immorality
And drunkness whilst Darlaston has gorged.

Markets dried up when the war with France ceased
And the massive loss of trade this entailed;
An old story - unemployment in peace,
In Darlaston, great misery prevailed.
The town cursed in ignorance and distress,
Reduced demand for gun locks that they made,
Descent into a pit of their own mess,
The decline of the gun lock making trade.

of four shillings or less, and very frequently he had no work at all. The greatest misery prevailed; those who had previously breakfasted on turkey, chicken or rabbit were now glad to get a bit of bread, bacon and cheese. Many who used to drink a bottle of wine at dinner now couldn't afford half a pint of beer and, in their ignorance and distress, would curse the peace and abuse their employers, working in sullenness and misery.

Millions of gun locks have been made here for the purpose of destroying our fellow creatures. During the French war they were worth from 8 to 15s each, and a good workman would get up two in a day.

They are now only worth 3 or 4s each, and a much better standard of work is required so that a man cannot make more than one a day. The workmen are incredibly ingenious, being able to forge almost anything on the anvil. Great quantities of iron, coal and free stone are found in this neighbourhood. There are many steel furnaces and forges for the supply of steel for the locks and springs which are made. The ground has also been so undermined that it is constantly falling in.

The language and terms of the workmen are such as but a few people can understand. Barbarisms, such as "*Um thinks as it's gooden like for wea*", "*Us*

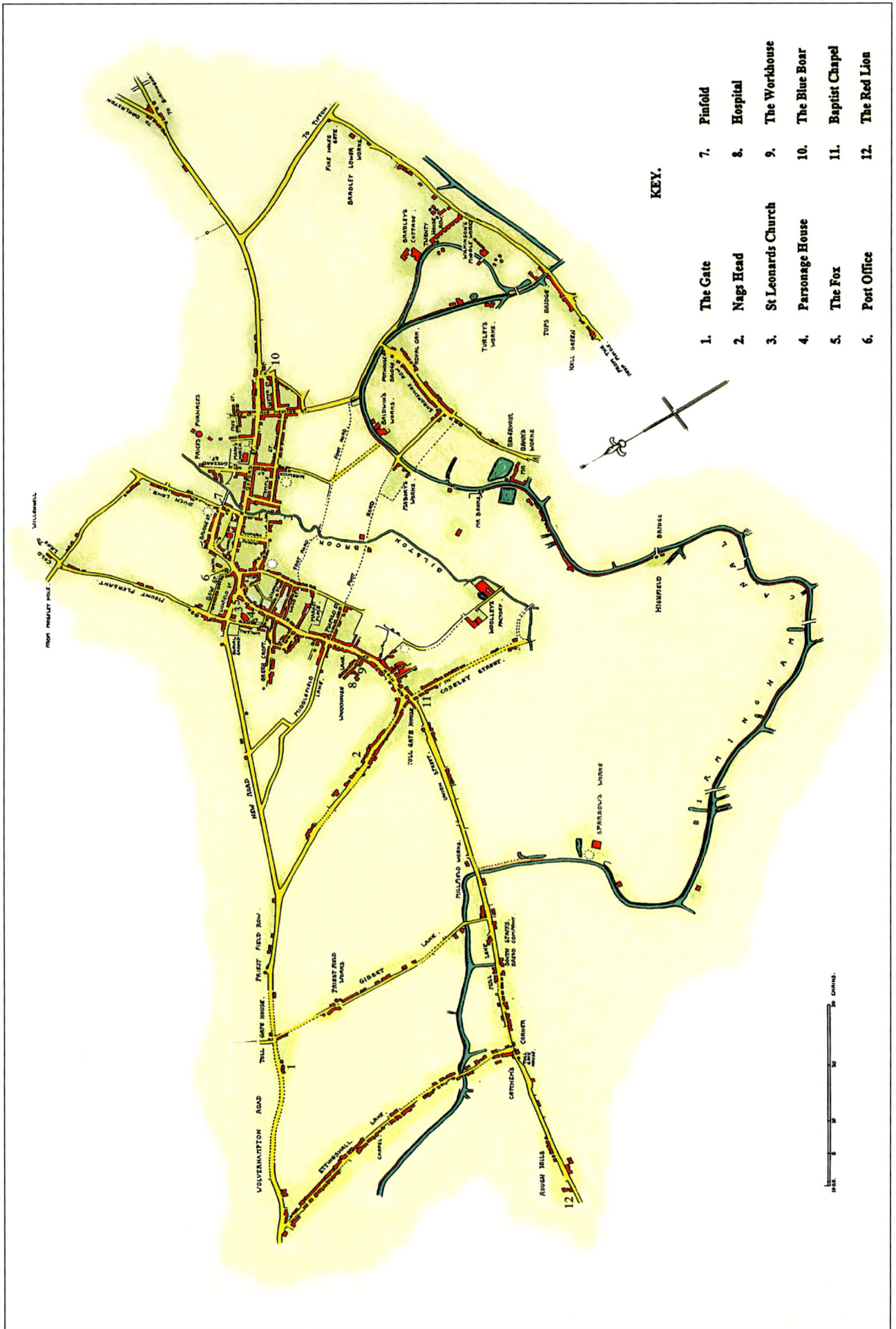

MAP OF BILSTON 1832 – THE YEAR OF THE CHOLERA OUTBREAK

KEY.

1. The Gate
2. Nags Head
3. St Leonards Church
4. Parsonage House
5. The Fox
6. Post Office
7. Pinfold
8. Hospital
9. The Workhouse
10. The Blue Boar
11. Baptist Chapel
12. The Red Lion

does the wark for they" and "Us have the *wark to daew* when *em awhants* it *deune* wael *far nobboddee abean* here *cono daou iten bun wae,*" are very common. Everything is alive when you hear them talk of their great works, their pits and their mines.

The women seem to lose their natural symmetry very early in life, and their mode of dress is generally so uncouth that they appear to be neither men nor women. There are plenty of women - the number of children we see proves that - but father, mother and children, seem to be without education or attention. The children play in the streets from the time that they can run until they go to the pit or the shop, and there they work till they have children themselves who do the same thing again.

About two and a half miles to the left of the railroad is the town of Bilston. It is a large, populous, and busy town in the parish of Wolverhampton. It stands on elevated ground and very advantageously situated, with the roads from London to Holyhead and from Birmingham to Manchester running through it, with the Birmingham and Wolverhampton Canal also passing close by. The place is ancient - under the Saxons it was called *Bilsretatum* and Billestune under the Normans. It is a long and straggling place, being considerably more than a mile in length but having only one good street. There are, however, many substantial and good-looking buildings, though the place is not at all regular or well-built. It has the usual signs of being a mining and iron manufacturing district containing a great number of small tenements for the workmen who, notwithstanding their comparatively good wages, are most regardless of comfort, either in their houses or selves. The population, which is constantly increasing, is now about 15,000.

The whole district around here is a mass of apparent disorganization, confusion and ruin. By day we see nothing but the remains of the disembowelling of the earth; heaps of stones, clay, coal, cinders and ashes, as if a volcano had erupted and covered the country with its lava; furnaces, chimneys, forges, and iron works, beds of burning coal, coal pits with their engines and apparatus,

and wagons conveying loads of stone and coal in every direction, attended by men, women and boys dressed as if they were accustomed to live in the earth. The whole is constantly enveloped in the gloom a one perpetual cloud of smoke, which bedims and darkens the country for miles around.

By night the countryside nearby is lit up by fires. On all sides the blazes of the furnaces, forges, coal pits, coke beds and lime kilns are seen glaring terrifically through the awful darkness. The rushing and roaring of the blasts of the furnaces, the thundering blows of the ponderous forge hammers, the clanking and crashing of the steam engines, pulley chains and ropes of the pits; the rattling and rumbling of the rolling mills and the clattering of the iron and stone all around give a stranger the most fearful and awful notions of the place. At night from a hill near the town, looking towards the town of Sedgley, nearly 200 blast furnaces for the smelting of iron from the ore may be seen, a sight unparalleled, probably, in any other part of the world.

There are two churches in Bilston. St. Leonard's stands in the centre of the town and is a large and spacious building, consisting of a Grecian Temple and a low tower. It is a modern structure, having been rebuilt in 1826. The living is in the gift of the resident householders, so that an induction causes an election according to the principles of household suffrage. St. Mary's, in Oxford-street, is a fine Gothic building of the style of the sixteenth century, with a handsome, square embattled tower crowned with pinnacles. The dissenting places of worship are a handsome Catholic chapel, in the low Gothic style in Oxford-street; a spacious Wesleyan Methodist chapel in Ettingshall Road; a New connexion Methodist chapel in Oxford-street; an Independent chapel in the same street; and a Baptist chapel in Wood Street. The Wesleyan Methodist chapel has a large burial ground attached to it, which has more graves probably than any other similar ground in the country.

The charities consist of the Town School, which has only one small endowment per annum, and the Cholera and Orphan School, which was built for

The 1832 Bilston Cholera Epidemic

What father should bury his own daughter?
His loving wife, brother, nieces or son?
A cholera outbreak, no clean water,
Facts we learned when we arrived at Bilston.
Thousands wiped out, whole families entire,
Stealing the lives of children who were killed.
Gliding past on our journey, the Wildfire,
The desolate cemeteries that were filled.

Bilston called out to God, themselves to save,
An army of angels on golden wings;
The answer was the silence of the grave,
Weakened workers in manufacturing.
Onwards, locomotive! Onwards, this train!
Why should innocent children have to die?
Onwards, Wildfire! Lets not endure this pain!
We journey forward under blackened sky.

the education of 450 orphans who lost their parents during the cholera outbreak in 1832. There are also funds for the relief of those widows and orphans who were left as such by the disease.

The working people are very rough and uncultivated in this district, but they are wonderfully civilized and moral compared with what they used to be. They were formerly extremely riotous and resorted to those brutal amusements of bear and bull baiting. Since the introduction of Methodism by John and Charles Wesley, there has been a marked improvement in the morals of the people, and the visitation of cholera in 1832 has also greatly contributed to the morality of the whole district. Cholera forms a very prominent feature in its modern history. In the months of August and September 1832, there were no less than 3,568 cases resulting in 742 deaths, and so raging and fatal was the disease that doctors, nurses, coffins, or graves could not be procured quickly enough. Out of the mining district's population of 160,000 were 10,000 cases of cholera and nearly 2,500 deaths.

The ground abounds with coal, iron, lime, sand, and stone, making it exceedingly valuable. In many

parts the coal strata, interspersed with pyrites, are so near the surface that decomposing water, causes a spontaneous combustion of the coal, which, in many instances, has been burning for more than half a century. As we walk over the land, we perceive volumes of smoke and vapour issuing from fissures in the ground. The chief trade is the manufacture of iron into bars, sheets, and hoops, and iron and tin plates. The quantity of iron made in the mining district of Staffordshire is immense - there are upwards of 200 smelting furnaces, and it is calculated that 2,000,000 tons of iron are produced annually.

The line now passes through a 50 feet deep cutting under the Birmingham Canal, which leaks through the arch. To the right is the manor of Bentley. Colonel Lane, who assisted Charles II after the battle of Worcester, lived here, and there was an oak felled nearby some years ago with a living toad in the centre of the trunk. Near to this spot in February 1838 a poor horse, which had strayed out of the fields, got on the road and the engine, in passing over it, was thrown off the line and ran into a field, killing the engineer. A horsebox was thrown over, and some horses killed, but no accident befell the passengers beyond being detained until the morning instead of getting home that same night. The fencing along the road has been better attended to since that time, the line carefully watched and guarded to prevent obstructions.

To the south west is the line of hills called Rowley Rag. It is composed of layers of basalt, and the stone is extensively employed in paving streets. A little further on we come to Willenhall Station. The town of Willenhall is a large and populous village of rather superior aspect, and lies on the direct road from Wolverhampton to Walsall. Willenhall is the same place as that which the Saxons called *Winehala*, a word denoting victory. The population is now about 7000.

The church, dedicated to St Giles, is a plain looking building, being merely a chapel-of-ease to the collegiate church of Wolverhampton. The living is a perpetual curacy in the gift of the resident freeholders. As well as the church, there are an Old and New Connexion Methodist chapel, and a Baptist chapel. There are not five pounds in benefactions for this place and, excepting Sunday schools, there are no means of instruction for the poorer class of children.

The town of Willenhall boasts the manufacturing of locks, bolts and latches as well as grid irons. The very smallest of locks are manufactured, along with the ponderous and massive ones used for gates and prisons. Some of the workmen are very ingenious; not long ago, one of them made half a dozen locks and keys, the weight of all of which did not exceed that of a sixpenny piece. It is also recorded that, in 1776, a 63 year old lock maker named Lees wrought a padlock and key lighter than a silver two penny coin. There are upwards of 400 lock and bolt-makers, and supposing they only make on average two gross a week each, they would manufacture upwards of 5,000,000 annually. At both this place and Wednesfield, locks and bolts are manufactured for all parts of the world. In good times, when trade is brisk, they are exported largely by means of the Wyrley and Essington Canal, but when trade is dull, the little masters are frequently obliged to take a few in a bag and carry them to the factories of Birmingham and Wolverhampton, even exchanging them for other articles before they can turn them into money.

The language of the lower classes can scarcely be understood by strangers. When speaking of education, they always pronounce school "*skeule*", and books "*baeukes*". They have had none of the first, and next to none of the second. Both here and at Darlaston there is a great deal of superstition among the uneducated. They believe in sights and sounds prior to and at the death of individuals, and a white dog is a favourite shape in which a ghost is supposed to exist. A wake, or feast, is held here in September, and the sports of bull baiting and cock fighting continue among the people.

We now pass over some level ground, and then through a cutting of gravel where smooth, round stones, called boulders, are sometimes found a ton in weight. The line then passes through a deep cutting, where on one side a thick stratum of coal is seen coming up to the surface with another of new red sandstone, and slate clay. On the left is a hamlet called Portobello, which has been entirely built since the opening of the line for the convenience of workmen and persons employed in one way or other on the railway. Here the railroad is a straight line for nearly two miles, and we can see under three arches, and a tunnel 180 yards in length, up to the Wolverhampton Station. This tunnel is formed for the purpose of passing under the Essington Canal.

To the right is the village of Wednesfield, from the Saxon "Woden's field", interpreted as the God of a War's place, or place of battle. Near here, or probably on this spot, a great battle was fought in 910 between the Saxons and the Danes, in which the Saxons were the victors. The name, it would seem, derives its origin from this fact.

Wednesfield is a pretty-looking village or township, in the parish of Wolverhampton and contains upwards of 2,000 inhabitants, who are employed in lock and bolt making, in the same way as the population of Willenhall. There is a chapel-of-ease, endowed with a few hundred pounds by the Gough family, of Perry Barr. There is also a small Methodist chapel. The people are almost without

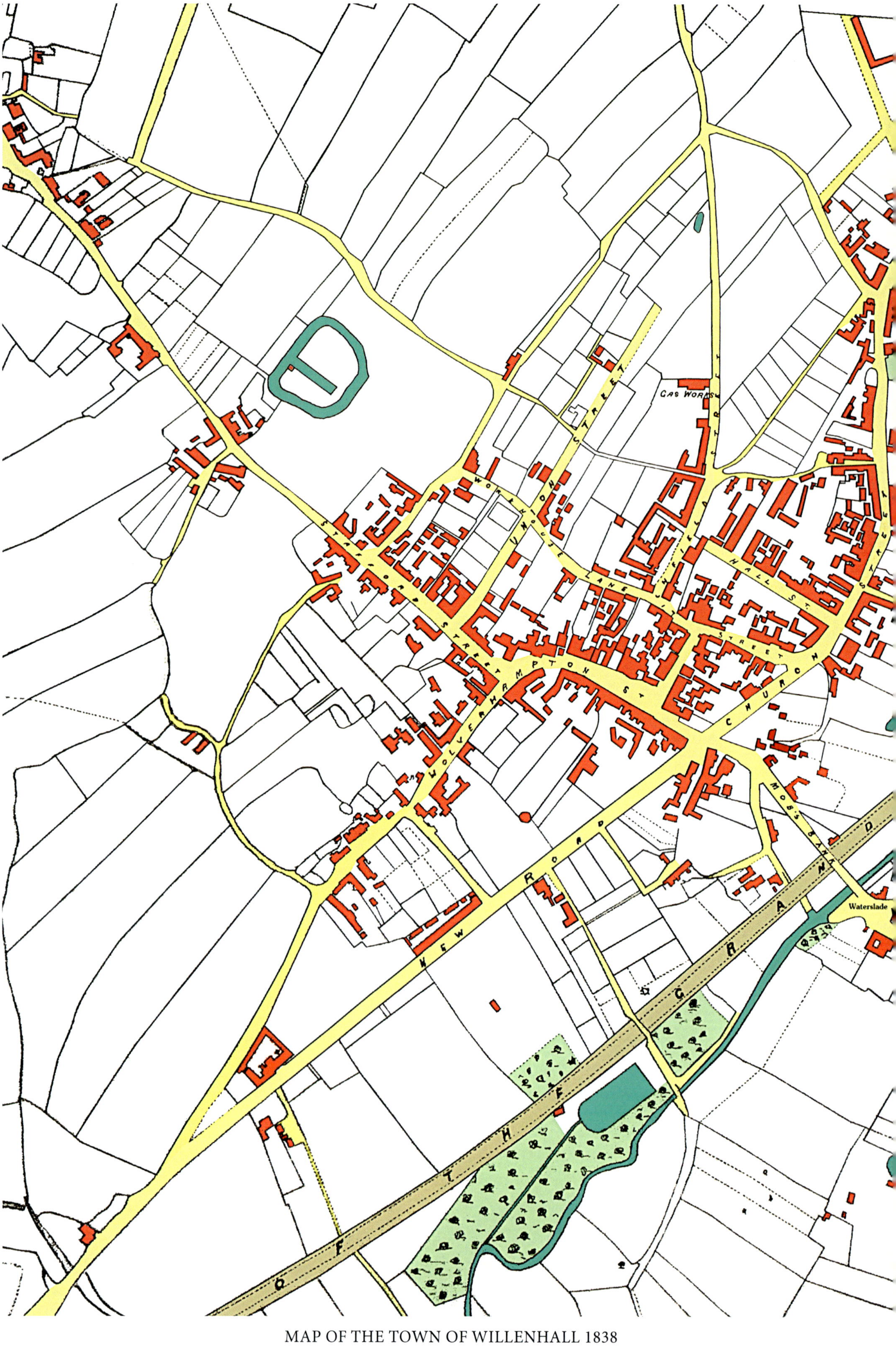
GAS WORKS
STAFFORD STREET
WOLVERHAMPTON ST
UNION STREET
WORKHOUSE LANE
HALL ST.
CHURCH
NEW ROAD
Waterslade
OF THE GRAND

MAP OF THE TOWN OF WILLENHALL 1838

THE CHURCH OF ST. GILES WILLENHALL

Rowley Hills –
From the Depths of the Earth

Geology matters, secrets in rocks,
An ancient history of what has been;
Keys to the past, bolted doors now unlocked,
Extinct fish, birds and mammoths can be seen.
Science of rocks is called geology,
Geologists detecting rocks for clues:
Earthquakes, volcanoes and ecology,
Climate change and how the land should be used.

Lulworth Cove and site of the Jurassic Coast
Or WrensNest in Dudley and trilobites;
Rowley Rag is the Black Country's proud boast,
A grey molten rock known as dolerite.
Rowley Hill's rich geodiversity
Was a pirate's map of buried treasure;
Employment and years of prosperity,
Quarries for the roadstone and CoalMeasures.

Roman soldiers came here on the Portway,
Rowley Rag on their roads in the Empire:
Rocks trodden down like a giant's causeway,
Footing for conquerors that does not tire;
In drystone walls, Roman coins have been found,
Emperor Galba, AD 69:
They came to extract rocks beneath the ground
And mineral ores in the ancient mines.

Rocks define the landscape, houses and walls,
Biodiversity on Rowley Hills;
Rowley Rag was once used for cannon balls,
At Dudley Castle and now for landfill.
Secrets in rocks, fossilised plesiosaurs,
Geologists uncovering the past:
How magma erupted from the earth's core,
Tropical forests and how rocks were cast.

Deserts covered Walsall, Bilston had dunes;
Bentley bathed on a Silurian shore.
Darlaston looked like the face of the moon,
Molten rocks welling up from the earth's core.
The advancing glaciers carved the land,
Flood waters depositing new sand beds;
Mammoths and reindeer on frozen grasslands,
Rowley Hills becoming a watershed.

Rocks tell the story of changing climate,
Rowley Rag quarried for the turnpike roads
On an industrial scale, aggregate,
Crushed rock, to help merchants transport their loads.
Rocks define the local environment,
They are used for cobblestones and paving,
Kerbstones, gutters, castles and tenements,
Rowley's quarries captured in engravings.

Willenhall Locks – (acrostic)
Dedicated to Councillors Diane & Sean Coughlan

Willenhall hands crafting little boxes of magic
Ingenuity and an industry
Locksmiths - secrets revealed with just a flick
Lovingly made, Willenhall's history.
England's finest, it was where locks were made
Now passed through on the Grand Junction Railway.
Honouring the past and Willenhall trade,
A manufacturing base with good pay
Locks - key to the present, door to the past,
Locksmiths - wizards who wove their skills and graft.

Locks are a treasure that will always last,
Our town, the beating heart of pride and graft,
Created a kitemark for global fame
Keys, steel production and coal from mine shafts,
Secured for Willenhall world-wide acclaim.

education and though they are very ingenious in their business they seem to possess nothing which can properly be called information. This place is on the banks of the Wyrley and Essington Canal, which lies over the tunnel, through which we pass. The tunnel is long enough to cause the railroad to appear dark as we go through it; on emerging from it we pass along two or three hundred yards of deep cutting, and arrive at Wolverhampton Station.

As this is one of the main stations on the line, all trains stop here whether departing or returning. A plentiful supply of water and coke is taken up to see us through to our destination. At the same time, the engine is checked over and the wheels are greased. As this station is of importance, there are always omnibuses and carriages ready to take passengers into the town of Wolverhampton.

Wolverhampton lies about a mile west of the line, and is a place of considerable importance. It is the Birmingham of Staffordshire, being the largest and most important place in its county. Seen from the line, it has all the appearance of being what it

really is - a busy, wealthy, and populous town. It is the last place of importance in this direction in the mining district, and consequently there is much beautiful and undisturbed natural scenery round about. Fields and gardens are close to it, on the north and east, and there is more of rural landscape in its neighbourhood than in that of any other town in the mining district.

It was anciently named only *Hanton or Hamton*, but in the tenth century, Wulfrana, the sister of King Edgar, founded a college here and endowed it so munificently that the place was named after her, and ultimately it changed from *Wul franis Hamton* to Wolverhampton.

The greater part of the town is composed of the common order of buildings for tradesmen and workmen, but many parts of the outskirts contain houses of great taste and elegance for those able to reside a distance from their business. It is about an equal distance to Birmingham, Lichfield, and Stafford, and there is so much traffic between Birmingham and Wolverhampton that they can

WOLVERHAMPTON FROM THE PENN ROAD 1831

almost be said to be united, the district being filled with mining works and factories, and interspersed with towns. The township contains about 28,000 inhabitants, but the parish, which is 30 miles in circumference, contains 15 hamlets and 50,000 inhabitants. There are some good shops here, and large factories and warehouses. Many of the inns and hotels are very extensive, showing that a great deal of commercial business is transacted. Wolverhampton was created a borough under the Reform Act, and sends two members to Parliament. The borough includes Bilston, Wednesfield, Willenhall, and Sedgley, and the number of voters is from 1,800 to 2,000.

The site of Wolverhampton, being on the direct line of road to Holyhead, Manchester and Liverpool, and communicating, as it does, with the great lines of the Midland canals, means that facilities for commerce and trade are very great and important.

There are several churches. The chief of them is the Collegiate, a handsome but very old and time-worn building, partly in the early decorated, but principally in the later style of English architecture. It is pleasantly situated on elevated ground towards the eastern side of the town, with a walk around it affording some very beautiful views. The church is built in the shape of a cross and has the internal as well as external signs of its Catholic origins. There is a handsome, lofty embattled tower, rising from the centre to a height of 120 feet and containing a fine set of bells and chimes. The sandstone it is composed of is very much blackened and decomposed by the effects of the atmosphere. St. John's Church, which is in the south west part of the town, is a handsome modern stone building with a lofty spire and a spacious burial ground. It is enclosed by a double row of trees but encompassed by a square of small houses, which destroy its effect. St. George's Church, on the Bilston Road, is a large building in the Doric order of Grecian architecture. St. Paul's, on the Worcester Road, is a very handsome Gothic building, with pinnacles but no spire. It was built by the clergyman who officiates. The chapels are numerous. The Roman Catholic chapel is a very handsome building, composed of a mixture of Gothic and Grecian architecture, and situated in North Street, adjoining Gifford House.

There is a Free Grammar School here, founded

in 1508 by Sir Stephen Jenyns, a native of the town, and Lord Mayor of London, who richly endowed it. The ancient and modern languages, the arts and sciences are taught. On two evenings in the week instruction is given to the boys of the working class in spelling and reading. The celebrated Dr Abernethy, the great founder of the indigestion system in medicine, and the no less celebrated Sir William Congreve, the inventor of the destructive war rockets, received their education at this school. The Blue Coat School receives a generous income, which is appropriated to the education of 150 boys and girls, of which 60 boys and 60 girls are clothed, and 6 of each sex are boarded and lodged in the school. The National School was built by subscription and is supported by annual contributions for the education of 250 boys and 200 girls. At the British School, at the Baptist chapel in Walsall Street, a considerable number of children are educated and there is reason to suppose that an extension of the principle of the school will take place, so that a greater number of the poorer class will have a better chance of being instructed

The Birmingham Canal, which comes up to the town of Wolverhampton, joins the Staffordshire and Worcester, along with the Wyrley and Essington Canals. There are coaches and omnibuses to all parts of the neighbourhood at every hour of the day. The manufacturers of this place consist of almost every kind of article that can be made of iron, brass or tin. The best of every kind of article that is made in each of the surrounding and neighbouring places is manufactured here: locks, bolts, chains, screws, hinges, latches, hammers, pincers, vices, gimlets, mills, traps, fire-irons, iron boxes, snuffers, nut-crackers, pliers, joiners' and carpenters' tools, etc. There is also another branch of manufacture, that of trays, waiters, thread baskets and caddies. The manufacturers of Wolverhampton and Birmingham are very similar, both being emporiums of the mining district. There are many iron furnaces and works in this neighbourhood, and of course plenty of coal and iron mines. There are also two worsted mills, and chemical works for the manufacture of sulphuric and nitric acids, and for Glauber's and Epsom salts. There are about 30 iron and coal masters, upwards of 300 lock and bolt makers, 50 key makers, and great numbers of steel toy makers, file makers, edge tool makers of every description and brass workers.

There are many very excellent hotels, the principal of which are the New Hotel, the Swan, the Star and Garter and the Peacock. The town is well lit with gas, and in the centre of the market place there is a large iron pillar with a lamp at the top. There is a corn and cattle market every Wednesday, which also supplies an abundance of every article for eating and wearing. There is also a market on Saturday for meat and vegetables. There is a fair on the 10th of July. The races, which are held on the Monday, Tuesday, and Wednesday nearest to the 12th of August, are very celebrated among the lovers of the turf. The course is a mile and a quarter circuit and is unrivalled for flatness of surface and fineness of sod. The Grand Stand is a very handsome building which cost many thousand pounds.

Wolverhampton Station is being made into a commercial depot - the railway company is building spacious warehouses and an engine-house capable of holding two or three engines. This accommodation and assistance will materially improve the commerce of the town and bring additional profit to the company. The line of road has hitherto been sparingly employed by the Wolverhampton merchants for want of a warehouse to deposit the goods and whenever an additional engine has been required at this part of the line, it had always had to be fetched from Birmingham.

On leaving Wolverhampton Station we pass along an embankment ranging from 9 to 25 feet high, and find the scenery of the peaceful countryside opening before us. On the right is a pretty little country house, Showhall, the residence of William Mannix, and a little further, on the same side, is Low Hill, the residence of R. S. Pountney. Almost opposite here is Oxley Hall, the birth-place of Mr Huskisson, the celebrated defender of free trade who lost his life on the Liverpool and Manchester Railway at its opening. Mr Hordern, a barrister, lives here now and, along with his lady, he takes great interest in, and is very attentive to, the welfare of the labouring class in the neighbourhood. There are several respectable houses belonging to Oxley, with Mr Taylor and Mr Warner, merchants of Wolverhampton, occupying two of them.

We pass under the bridge which supports the road to Bushbury Hall and the village, with its little church and school, comes into view. The church is very pretty and as the neighbouring gentry having supplied it with an organ, the service is more pleasing than that of most village churches. A school has been built by Miss Hinks where, by means of subscriptions and the payment of a penny a week from each scholar, 60 children are educated and clothed. Bushbury Hall is near the church, and is one of the many places in this neighbourhood where Charles I was secreted. A chair is preserved here in which the king sat. On the top of Bushbury Hill, the Clee Hills, the Abberley, Wolverley, and Malvern Hills, in Worcestershire, the Wrekin, in Shropshire, and some of the mountains in Wales, are visible. By night the iron Works in Shropshire are to be seen blazing.

A little further to the east is Moseley Court, the residence of G. T. Whitgreave. Charles I was concealed here for some time after the battle of Worcester and the present building is in a modern style, the grounds laid out tastefully. Still further on in the same direction is Moseley Hall, an old building, a great part of which has been turned into barns and stabling. It is said that Charles I was also hidden here and Thomas Holyoake resides in this place at present. There is much pleasant rural scenery around it, and nothing occurs to break the silence or disturb the tranquility of this pastoral haunt. The old Moseley Hall is one of the most thoroughly ancient houses in the kingdom. On the west is the hamlet of Ford Houses, where there is a mill turned by Wybaston Brook, which runs under the road.

The neighbouring countryside is of Arcadian tranquility. The land is owned by gentlemen farmers who richly and carefully cultivate it, adorning it with well-built and pleasantly arranged houses. The rushing and clattering engine, with its thundering train, passes by rapidly 14 times a day, putting everything into commotion for a few minutes, but it is soon gone and leaves no trace behind it; all is soon quiet again as if no disturbance had ever occurred.

To the east, after passing Moseley Court, is Hilton Hall, the seat of Colonel Graham. The surrounding countryside is very beautiful, abounding in pastures, shady lanes and brooks. The Hall is a handsome brick building, composed of a centre and two wings, and has an elegant balustrade around it. It stands on a beautiful lawn, surrounded by lovely grounds which are protected by a deep moat. In front of the house is a lofty ascent, at the summit of which stands a Norman tower from which there is a most extensive and delightful view of upwards of 100 miles round, from Derbyshire into Wales. The grounds and gardens are laid out with great taste, and the more beautiful parts are seen as we go over the road towards the house. Laurels and acacias adorn the walks and a choice collection of rare shrubs and plants are tastefully laid out over the grounds. A large and lofty greenhouse, surmounted with a dome, is by the side of the Hall. The park is not very large, but it is in admirable order. To the left is a fine, winding sheet of water, covered with trees and adorned with little islands. The whole scene is a paradise not easily equaled and rarely surpassed.

We pass over another embankment, varying from 8 to 20 feet in height, and to the west, although out of view, is Wrottesley Hall - the seat of Lord Wrottesley -and the adjoining village of Codsall. We pass under Cross Green Bridge, the way to Cannock Chase, and come to Paradise Bridge. Here, to the left and at some distance, is Chillington Park and Hall, the seat of T. W. Gifford, a gentleman of a very ancient family, and who is often termed one of the "fine old English gentlemen." He is very fond of the popular sports of the country, and was the principal person who established the race at Wolverhampton. Passing his seat we see the hamlet of Coven, where the poor people make their living by lock making, but which is so reduced in price that it is only with difficulty they can do so. The road to the park is up

CHILLINGTON

Chillington Hall - An Arcadian Tranquility

When the setting sun is softening down,
Enveloping sky full of foundry sparks:
We leave all the manufacturing towns
And journey to Chillington Hall and Park;
Into calm inspiring hues of twilight,
Beautiful stillness, quiet of the country.
Chillington Hall, a magnificent sight,
It's an Arcadian tranquillity.

The Hall is bordered by well maintained lawns,
Pastureland, shady lanes and charming brooks.
As night slowly fell we saw deer with fawns,
Nocturnal shelter in their leafy nooks.
Entrance was gained down tree-lined avenues,
This English Eden in serenity:
Over this paradise was lovely views,
It's an Arcadian tranquillity.

The village of Brewood, left of the line,
With quiet and luxuriant country around;
An English oasis, free from coal mines,
The church has well tended burial grounds.
In Heaven and Earth there is no conflict,
All is one in peaceful prosperity:
The opposite in the mining district,
It's an Arcadian tranquillity.

A delightful contrast to poor Bilston,
This haunt is a paradise unsurpassed.
Contemplative beneath the fading sun,
Shadows of evening lengthen, night is cast.
Over the trees rises Brewood's church spire,
Moths replace butterflies in shrubberies:
We must take our rest, as must the Wildfire,
It's an Arcadian tranquillity.

an avenue two miles in length, adorned on either side with lofty trees and intersected by the passage of the Grand Junction Canal.

The Grand Junction is one of the finest pieces of work, and one of the most beautiful sights that the country affords. It is cut out to a great depth, and the sides of the banks are covered with gorse, so as to resemble the banks of a river in a forest. Several very beautiful and lofty bridges cross it, from whence the canal far below can be seen, with its slow and solitary barges and silent attendants. The park, with the village spire of Brewood rising over the surrounding trees, and the quiet and luxuriant surrounding countryside, forms a scene which is impossible to behold without a deep sense of pleasure. If seen at evening when the rays of the setting sun are softening down into the calming hues of twilight, few could leave without reluctance. The Hall is a fine mansion, composed of a handsome centre, with pillars, and two large wings, and stands in the midst of a beautiful park, containing delightful shrubberies and grounds.

The canal leads to Brewood, a village to the left of the line and one of the prettiest little spots in the county. It is situated on a slight eminence, but is almost completely hidden on every side by trees. There are many respectable houses in it, and the labourer's lot seems to benefit from the cleanliness and comfort of his more wealthy and fortunate neighbours. The church, dedicated to the Virgin Mary, is a very handsome Saxon building, with a lofty spire in excellent condition, and stands in the midst of a large, clean, well-tended burial ground.

Somerford Park is the residence of the Hon. Edward Monckton. The river Penk runs through the grounds, forming an elegant cascade and a fishing dam. The grounds are elegantly laid out, and the road from Brewood lies through the park. The sequestered and contemplative appearance of this spot is a very delightful contrast to some of the places of the mining district.

We now cross the Staffordshire and Worcestershire Canal via a handsome and strong iron bridge, and the village of Slade Heath is seen down in the vale to the west. The Stafford and Wolverhampton Road is close by the side of the line, which it crosses twice, keeping by its side all the way to Penkridge and most of the way to Stafford. The village of Pendeford is a very pretty object on the left, and far to the right, nearly behind us, there is a beautiful hill surmounted by a handsome clump of trees and a windmill. There is a good view to the east from here, reaching as far as Penkridge and Cannock Chase, a dark moor of many miles in extent belonging to the Marquis of Anglesey. We now arrive at Four Ashes Station.

The hamlet of Four Ashes lies a few hundred yards to the left of the station, and the villages of Shareshill and Featherstone are to the right. As soon as we pass the station we have a good view of the Wrekin in Shropshire, seen from the Standeford embankment which is six miles long and, in some places, is very high above the neighbouring ground. We soon pass through an excavation which shuts out our view, but from the summit of the embankment there is nothing to be seen except the dark heath of Cannock and a few scattered farm houses. We next come to Spread Eagle Station.

Here, the old Roman way, Watling Street, crosses the road from the Four Crosses to the Four Ashes, and on to Chester. This road is one of the ways by which the Romans traversed the length and breadth of the island. There appears to have been four principal roads: Watling Street, Ikenield Street, Ermine Street and the Fosse Way. Watling Street, the one which we are now at, runs from Dover to London, where the name and site of the road is still retained. From the capital it runs to St. Albans, in Hertfordshire, and thence through Buckinghamshire, Northamptonshire, Warwickshire and Staffordshire, on to Chester and North Wales. Ikenield Street begins at Teignmouth in Northumberland and passes through Durham into Yorkshire via Bolsover, through Derbyshire via Chesterfield, Derby, and thence into Warwickshire via Sutton Coldfield and Aston to Alceston, then to Stow, in Gloucestershire, and to Winchester and Southampton in Hampshire.

About three miles to the right is Four Crosses, a small village on the old Watling Street route, and on the direct road from Birmingham to Chester. It is the only place in the neighbourhood where post horses can be obtained. Before the railroad was established it was frequently visited by travellers, but now few go there. Four fine roads meet at this place, and there are two or three handsome houses, but the village is very small, hardly worth noticing except for its site on the great Roman road from London to North Wales. The surrounding countryside contains many delightful spots, where the gentry reside.

A little further on, and still more to the east, is the village of Cannock. A very pretty place, it is most charmingly situated on the edge of the great moor or chase. There are many large and handsome houses, and all the buildings, including the cottages, have a very clean and orderly appearance. It is one of those places that makes us feel the beautiful stillness of the country, whilst still having population and houses enough to give us the feeling of safety in a town. The parish is very extensive, comprising about 20,000 acres of which nearly half is encompassed by Cannock Chase. It contains 3,116 inhabitants.

The Church, which is in the middle of the village, is an old Gothic building. Its tower is ancient, and retains on its corners the remains of griffin and dragon heads, which were formerly intended as objects of terror on country churches. The church yard is a beautiful rural spot and contains many gravestones, which are curious both in their sculpture and the inscriptions upon them.

There is a small, independent chapel, built in the Saxon style, with the minister's house close by. It is situated in the midst of very pleasant grounds; a good garden is attached, which is kept in very pretty order. The minister is one of the Home Missionaries for the county of Stafford. There is a small parish school, which has a trifling endowment, and a National School built by Mrs Walhouse of Hatherton Hall and at which 200 children are educated at her expense.

There is a very excellent and exceedingly comfortable inn, The Crown, the landlady of which is a very superior woman in person, manners and general information. A short distance from

here is Hatherton Hall, the residence of Mrs Walhouse, the mother of Lord Hatherton. The house is a plain, modern structure, with beautiful grounds and an extensive park in front. One part of the garden is very interesting, being devoted to the cultivation of bees. The grounds of this little enclosure are covered with the sweetest heathers and thymes, and a large shell of water is filled with pebbles to enable the bees to drink. A bell stands in the poultry yard around which, when it is rung, the poultry and pigeons assemble to be fed. It is very curious that the noise of the bell, which the poultry and pigeons would be frightened at and fly away from in their natural state, should call the domesticated birds together.

Close by is Cannock Chase, a large expanse of moor upwards of 12 miles long and from two to five in breadth. Here we obtain a very fine view of the surrounding country, to the extent of 50 and perhaps even 100 miles. The chase contains more than 30,000 acres of land on which grass, heath, ling, gorse, and ferns grow and flourish, lending beauty to this otherwise dreary desert. A great portion of the flora which grew here was destroyed by a fire caused by a woman who once went on the moor to gather and burn fern. The hot weather meant the dry shrubs of the forest ignited, and hundreds of acres were destroyed. A burnt tree is seen from a great distance due to its blackness when the other trees are in leaf.

Here there is a majestic sweep of hills, from the tops of which, in fine weather, a number of beautiful horses can be seen training at Hednesford, a hamlet enclosed on the common whose inhabitants are employed entirely in husbandry. The wildness and great extent of the chase, the variety of light and shade on its hills and valleys and the few and distant lonely cottages seen on the hill slopes render the scene one of the most romantic in the country. Lichfield, Stafford, and Rugeley are to one side, Cannock, Brewood, and Wolverhampton the other. The valleys lie basking in the sunshine, or darkly shrouded in gloom at our feet. The woods of past centuries, clad in sternness at a distance, rise in solemn grandeur on one side; on the other

Cannock Chase - Winds of Heaven Blow Free

The Wildfire journeys on through Staffordshire
Fleeing the manufacturing district,
Squalor, human misery and conflict.
The Grand Junction Railway, bound for Cheshire,
Riding the rails before we disappear,
Our free passage that no one can restrict.
This journey now takes us to wild country:
Cannock Chase, where winds of Heaven blow free.

A wildness, scarcely equalled in England,
Where Kings of Mercia hunted game.
A royal park given a Saxon name,
Haunt of mounted nobles, hawks on their hand,
Hunting the stag, boar and wolf on this land.
Nature holds sway and burns like a green flame,
Undisputed in its stern majesty:
Cannock Chase, where winds of Heaven blow free.

Woods, heaths and valleys are in this domain
Set in 30,000 acres of moor
Where nature is red in tooth and in claw.
Magnificant views are seen from the train,
Mapped out before us, all England is lain,
Where the scudding clouds obey their own laws.
All this was revealed in its wild beauty:
Cannock Chase, where winds of Heaven blow free.

The valleys lie basking in the sunshine,
Variety of light and shade on hills;
Distant cottages and a water mill,
All of this observed from the railway line.
Subterranean workings in coal mines,
It is almost as if time has stood still:
These woodlands have been here for centuries:
Cannock Chase, where winds of Heaven blow free.

The human world, one of heartache and pain:
Escape it and lie down beneath the oaks,
Whose branches conceal you in their green cloaks.
In their bowers is a woodland refrain,
A cuckoo, herald when summertime reigns
And all my childhood dreams the bird awoke,
Greenwood adventures fill my memory:
Cannock Chase, where winds of Heaven blow free.

At a distance, clad in sternness and frowns,
The Wrekin and Shropshire Mountains are seen
And the farmlands of Lichfield mapped in green.
Stretched out before us are Staffordshire`s towns,
A panoramic view in green and brown,
Boarded by the horizon, all serene:
From the Wildfire, all of this I did see:
Cannock Chase, where winds of Heaven blow free.

THE WREKIN

the counties of Derbyshire, Nottinghamshire and Leicestershire, with their hundreds of villages, are seen mapped out until the view meets the horizon some 50 miles away. To the west, the dome of the Wrekin, the Shropshire mountain, rises in dark and awful majesty, and near it is the line of the Clee and Abberley Hills joining earth to sky. The winds blow upon us with a power that we seldom experience on land, and the whole scene is one of singular and stern beauty scarcely equaled in the wildness of its character by any other portion of England.

While we are engaged in contemplating the grandeur of the surrounding landscape, a company of hunters passes by, mounted on spirited steeds following a pack of beautiful hounds, giving us a faint notion of the grandeur of former times when this was a royal chase, and kings and nobles with their feudal trains passed by like gods of the earth. Here, ages ago, the kings of Mercia, under the Saxon Heptarch, hunted the stag, and to this day the nobles of the land follow the same practice.

Near to Cannock, on the Walsall road, are the ironworks of Mr Gilpin where edge tools of all kinds are forged and ground. The rapidity of the hammer's motion, which first forges the iron, is fascinating to the bystander. Several hundred strokes are given by some of the hammers in a minute; an instrument is manufactured with a rapidity that we can scarcely conceive. In the grinding department, every lathe is brilliantly lit with a shower of sparks, a true spectacle to behold at night. Near these manufacturing works are remains of pits and former places of manufacture, and the old Roman road, Watling Street, passes by.

About five miles from Lichfield is the seat of the Marquis of Anglesey, the Lord of the Manor. The Park is called Beaudesert- the "beautiful wild". Beautiful indeed it is! The Park consists of glorious hills and dells of wood, remains of moats and encampments, mounds and dykes, platforms and esplanades, all covered with the richest shrubberies and trees, carpeted with the flowers. The hall, an old Elizabethan building, is almost an exact copy of Aston Hall at Birmingham and has a fine and extensive lawn before it, with lofty hills to the rear. Herds of graceful deer of huge size roam this beautiful domain, many with antlers a yard and a half high, giving them a stately and imposing appearance. The spires and towers of Lichfield Cathedral, pointing to the skies, appear amid the trees at a distance, and the towns of Rugeley and Long seem to sleep peacefully amid the quiet and

BEAUDESERT

Beaudesert - Amongst the Bluebells
Dedicated to Bernard M Jackson

Beaudesert stands proud under a blue sky
As if held aloft by towering trees;
Summer birds give voice to their melodies
Around young dreams, in bluebells, where I'd lie.
The winged dreams of childhood spread and did fly
But those young dreams live on in memories;
Although blown forward like a gust of leaves,
Childhood happiness is caught on a sigh.

Overlooking the fields, my woodland glade
Remains rooted, although swift years have passed
And winter has serried each blade of grass,
Each secret leafy den where I once played,
In dappled sunlight, fleeting like a shade.
Childhood's end has come, I'm a parent now,
Children's laughter stirs dreams and they allow
A revisit to where young feet have strayed.

calmness of the rural scenery. There are many Gothic farm houses and cottages adorning the grounds that show both the taste and benevolence of the proprietor. Many areas are possessed by the cottagers, who merely pay an acknowledgment to the noble owner, and many farms on the common have been formed from the waste land on such easy terms that they are as good possessions as freeholds.

The country around is most delightful, picturesque and romantic. Lanes wind through hills and valleys amid pasture and cultivated ground, and the abundance of beautiful cattle and warbling birds add interest to the scenery. It is in all respects one of the most thoroughly old English places that can be visited and it is worth any person's while to pay their respects to it. On the hill on the common resides Mr Brindley, a hospitable farmer of the good old sort. If kindness and respectful attention deserve to be immortalized, posterity will give this family honorable distinction.

After passing the Spread Eagle Station Rodbaston Hall, the seat of Mr Holland, is seen on the right, but there is nothing particularly worthy of our attention.

The remains of Pilaton Hall, formerly the residence of the Lyttleton family, are also on the same side but the building is now only used as the residence for labourers. On the west of the line is Stretton, a village that contains about 300 inhabitants and has a small, modern church. Closer to us is Stretton Hall, the residence of Mr Monckton. It is a neat, modern mansion with a spacious lawn and surrounded by beautiful plantations. The site of Stretton is believed to have been a Roman station and implements from the age have been discovered in the neighbourhood. The Roman Pennocrucium is supposed to have been somewhere close, but the name of Penkridge causes some to conclude that it was placed there instead. A mill is turned by the river Penk, which twice crosses the road between Wolverhampton and Penkridge, running through the most delightful parts of this beautiful tract. On the same side is Water Eaton, a village on the banks of the Penk. Congreve, another hamlet nearby, was the birthplace of the celebrated Bishop Hurd, who was first installed at Lichfield then promoted to Worcester.

LICHFIELD CATHEDRAL

The line passes through occasional cuttings of gravel resting on sandstone, some of which is of very fine quality. There is a water station close at hand supplying engines if needed, and near to it stands a very neat, modern brick building, the residence of Mr Hazeldine. We now come to the Penkridge embankment, in some places upwards of 40 feet high, and can see Cannock Chase far off to the right, black and lowering. Teddesley Hall, the seat of Lord Hatherton, gleams through the thick woods to the north beyond Penkridge. The spire of the little church at Stretton lies far to the west, and down below us in the vale is one of the most picturesque views that a tourist can behold.

The object that first attracts the attention is Penkridge Church, a handsome Gothic building standing in a peaceful and beautiful churchyard adorned with neat tombstones and well-tended mounds. Its fine Norman tower is in excellent repair and perfect preservation. Behind is the town of Penkridge and on each side are farm houses and cottages, surrounded by yew trees and cypresses, adding solemnity to the rural scenery. The church is so inviting in its appearance that you can hardly pass by without visiting it, but it is time well spent. There is a main entrance by the tower and one on each side of the aisles. The interior is very handsome, in good repair, and extremely clean and comfortable. The stalls for the choir show that the church was once collegiate, and we find that in the days of King John there was a Dean and 13 honorary canons. The college was dissolved by Edward VI but is still what is called a Royal Peculiar, having in its jurisdiction the three chapelries of Dunston, Coppenhall and Stretton. The church is supposed to have been founded by King Edgar in the year 964. It was repaired, and the interior renewed and enlarged by the addition of a north gallery in the year 1831. Eight bells were placed in the tower at the same time and the ancient monuments of the Lyttleton family, in the chancel, were re-chiselled and polished, so that they appear in a high state of preservation. The living is a perpetual curacy, in the gift of the impropriator, the Right Hon. E. J. Lyttleton, and the incumbent holds visitations, probate courts, and licenses, the clergy of those four places being within his jurisdiction.

On the left hand of the line, just before we come to the church, is the parsonage house, one recently built on an acre of land donated by the patron, who also contributed 33,000 bricks towards its construction.

The river Penk flows under the road a little further on, winding through some deliciously green meadows over which is a viaduct of seven arches. Each spans 30 feet, and is 37 feet high. The lofty position of the passenger gives a perfect panorama,

PENKRIDGE CHURCH FROM THE GRAND JUNCTION RAILWAY

and as he proceeds new beauties are successively opened to him. We have now arrived at Penkridge Station. The river winds gracefully along on both sides, and to the right is the old bridge over which we pass to the town. Penkridge is a very pretty, neat and clean place in the midst of an agricultural district on the Stafford Road.

Though it neither possesses any manufacture nor is a market town, it is however a busy place, a great amount of traffic carried by the road on which it stands. It contains many respectable houses and two or three inns, the chief of which is the Lyttleton Arms, a large, commodious and excellent house, once frequently visited by stage coaches and commercial travellers. Around 20 coaches used to pass through this town every day, but since the opening of the railway they have all been discontinued, and now a travelling carriage is seldom seen. The population is about 3,000. A Methodist chapel stands next to the church and there is an excellent National School, conducted on Bell's system, where 250 children are educated and partly clothed. The rest of the maintenance expenses are obtained by subscriptions, principally from Lord Hatherton. A Sunday school is connected with the Church, and one with the Methodist chapel.

Three fairs are held here: for horses and cattle on the 30th of April, another on the 2nd of September, and the third on the 10th of October. There is a horse race in September which attracts a good deal of notice.

About two miles to the north east is Teddesley Hall, the seat of Lord Hatherton. We cross the winding Penk over a rural bridge and, proceeding through rich pastures, arrive at the park. We pass through a deep forest of fine, old trees and, having gained the summit of the rising ground by an extensive winding road, we at length arrive at the front of the hall, a large, modern, square stone building with out-houses to the rear and partially enclosed by pleasure grounds. In front, and on each side, is a magnificent sweep of lawn bounded by hills and dales covered by woods and plantations. To the rear is Cannock Chase in its solitary grandeur and to the left front are the towns of Penkridge and Acton,

the towers of their churches rising conspicuously. At the foot of the park runs the Penk, winding its devious way through the meadows, giving beauty to the scenery around.

Lord Hatherton was raised to the peerage soon after Lord Grey's retirement from office. He was one of the members for Staffordshire for 22 years, and held the responsible office of Secretary for Ireland during the latter part of Lord Grey's administration. Since his elevation to the peerage he has taken little part in the political affairs of the day. To the right is the village of Acton Trussel, a pretty rural place, with its small Norman church, fertile fields and scattered cottages. Still further on to the right, is the vale of Shugborough, where the majestic Trent receives the wandering Sow, and flows through a rich undulating country amid mansions of great elegance and grandeur. We next pass the village of Dunston, where an old stone Norman tower is combined with a dirty, smoky, miserable little brick-built church. Nothing can be in more wretched taste. It gives an appearance of misery to the whole place.

On the left, at some distance from the line, is the Village of Bradley, where there is an ancient Gothic Church, and a good Free School which was erected and endowed in the time of Edward VI. The boys of the Village are taught to read and write their own language, along with the classics if they choose.

There are many villages and hamlets on the west side of the line, but none are of any consequence or interest until Castle Church, noticed on arrival at Stafford. To the east is Brocton Hall, the seat of W. F. Chetwynd. It is a very pleasant place close to the borders of the Shugborough valley, where the trees and shrubs flourish delightfully and the country is rich in pasture and meadow. Still further to the right, on the Lichfield road and by the side of the romantic Trent is Shugborough Hall, the classic and elegant seat of the Earl of Lichfield. The scenery before arrival prepares us for one of those treats which, when seen, is not easily forgotten. The Sow, having meandered along irrigating and fertilizing the land, falls into the Trent and assists in swelling the flow of this noble river. Down in a vale before us we catch a glimpse of the park and hall and, after passing by

SHUGBOROUGH HALL

Sonnet for Lord Anson
(Shugborough Hall)

Commodore Lord Anson, the British fleet,
He sailed the seven seas beneath his mast;
Did his duty, his destiny was cast.
Shugborough Hall his home, Lichfield his seat:
Captured Spanish gold, his life was complete.
An adventurer for the British Crown,
Plundered Spanish galleons, his renown
And the bravest man you could ever meet.

He retired to gardens in Staffordshire,
Follies on his land with lofty ascent;
Chinese temples and ancient monuments,
While he pined for glories of yesteryear.
He became a recluse, rarely appeared,
In nostalgia for the South China Seas:
Crash of surf and sails snapping in the breeze,
Childless, salt water in his lonely tears.

a small village, we come to Tixall, between which place and the park the Trent flows. The park gates are on the opposite side, and the river is here so shallow that it is easily crossed. On arriving at the park we immediately perceive that there is much taste manifested in the culture and arrangement of the grounds. Passing through a portion of the walks and drives we see the gardens on our right, and the park, with the river flowing through it, on our left. There is a beautiful platform in front of the house, and beyond is a dark and shadowy wood intermixed with groves and bowers. The hall is a light and elegant building, after the manner of a Roman villa, with a square centre and fine portico, and is adorned with eight massive, fluted Ionic columns, relieved by two light wings graced with the drapery of laurels and other delightful evergreens.

The entrance is accessed by a handsome flight of step to a hall adorned with a profusion of statues of Grecian beauties and busts of celebrated personages. The walls of the anti-room and dining-room are covered with paintings, of which Susanna and the Elders by Guido, a picture of the Earl as a child, and two works of his fellow children by the late Lady Anson are particularly remarkable. The saloon looks out on a grass plot and a branch of the river which has been widened into a fine sheet of water. By its edge stand some picturesque ruins of the former hall, consisting of archways, Gothic windows and broken pillars. The library, which contains a fine collection of books, is a most enchanting place, being adorned with everything which is useful and pleasing. The grounds and gardens are laid out with great taste and elegance. They are ornamented with temples, statues and a beautiful arch, the monument in memory of Commodore Lord Anson who had the honor of conveying the Queen of George the III across the Channel. There is a piece of a sculpture by Schemecher, which is much admired and consists of two lovers gazing on a shepherd, who points to a tomb. The greenhouse, which was once a private theatre, contains a rich variety of plants and some beautiful pieces of sculpture. There is also a Chinese temple of very considerable beauty in which we might almost imagine ourselves in China.

The park consists of many hundreds of acres of highly cultivated land, richly skirted with woods and bounded on one side by the dark and bleak Cannock Chase. The noble Earl is a great farmer, cultivating upwards of 2000 acres himself, and the whole appearance of the estate is testament to his skills and taste.

A little further on is Tixall Hall, the residence of Sir T. Clifford Constable. The hall and park stand upon the beautiful angle lying between the junction of the Trent and Sow. The hall, situated on the rise of a fine sylvan lawn, is a plain and substantial modern building, with a handsome portico of Doric architecture ornamented with a majestic figure of a lion on one side and a lioness on the other. Close to the south wing of the hall is a Roman Catholic chapel, a modem Gothic building. Near this place is Tixall Heath, where Sir William Chetwynd was murdered by some ruffians hired by Sir H. Stanley during the reign of Henry VII. The parish church of Tixall is a pretty little building used as a rectory. The Staffordshire and Worcestershire Canal passes through the park, where it assumes the form of a large and beautiful lake, a reservoir for the waters of the canal as well as adding to the attractions of the domain.

The Penkridge embankment, a mile long, is in many places between 30 and 40 feet above the level of the meadows and affords a fine view of the surrounding scenery. We pass through a cutting nearly a mile in length and come to the Dunston embankment. The speed of the train gradually increases as we leave Wolverhampton, and passes thence to Stafford at the rate of 40 miles an hour. The sight of the trains passing down this inclined plane with such flying speed at night is one that few have the opportunity of beholding. There is probably nothing in machinery which gives us so complete a notion of the tremendous effect of power as such a fearful sweeping along of a rapid train. It seems, while rushing by with the velocity of the wind, to be the very acme of mechanical force, and when we recollect that all this power is produced by the mere expansion of water we are at a loss which to admire most - the invention of man or the adaptation of the laws of nature to such purposes.

Shugborough Hall (England`s Paradise)

We head to Lord Lichfield`s elegant seat,
The River Trent crosses our carriage road.
Shugborough Hall is Lord Lichfield`s abode,
Commodore Lord Anson, the British fleet.
The carriageway opens up to a treat,
Travel fatigue blows away heavy loads
And our carriage speeds up, no time to waste:
This a stately home of beauty and taste.

Once seen it's not forgotten easily:
It is built like Arcadia in style;
Enchanting gardens to loiter awhile,
Shugborough Hall is a place of beauty.
The River Trent flows through this rich country
Irrigating farmland around for miles.
It's difficult not to be affected,
In awe of this majesty erected.

A wood intermixed with groves and bowers,
The Hall is built like a Roman villa,
Adorned with fluted Iconic pillars.
Carpets of green sward, spangled with flowers,
Boarded by fir trees which rise like towers.
At work, gentlemen farmers and millers,
All at work in this tranquil scenery:
England`s paradise amongst greenery.

TIXALL HALL

This part of the road presented a singular phenomenon in the making of its embankment. For weeks, all the matter which the workmen laid upon it sank in and disappeared, the ground being boggy. It was a curious problem to know what became of the materials, and it was at length discovered that a neighbouring field rose and presented a considerable hill so that, from some curious and unexplained cause, the materials employed pushed up the land in that direction. However, the embankment was at length effected, and it is now as sound and good as any other portion of the railroad. Another part of the line nearer to Stafford, occasioned very great trouble to the engineer, a bog swallowing up all which was thrown into it for a considerable time, without causing a rise anywhere.

The village of Coppenhall lies on the left hand of the railroad along with the remains of several halls, as well as the site of an ancient Priory in the neighbourhood of Shredicote, but there is nothing worthy of special notice. The towers of Stafford Castle are seen most of the way from Penkridge, and as we come nearer to it we perceive that the building, though modern, is in an ancient style and stands on one of the hills which the Saxons used for their fortresses. We now arrive at Stafford Station.

It possesses an engine house, where a spare engine is kept always ready for service so that, if the trains do not arrive as they are expected, news of the cause can soon be obtained, and if any extra power is wanted, the engine is attached to the train to assist. Without delays, the first class train usually runs from Birmingham to Stafford in an hour.

The castle lies about a mile to the west, the town about half a mile to the east of the station. Omnibuses from the town's two principal inns attend to convey passengers, and in going there we cross the River Sow, on which the borough stands. Stafford is a borough, market town and parish in the southern division of the Hundred of Pirehill, but having separate jurisdiction. It is the capital of the county of the same name, and is situated on the River Sow, six miles from where it meets the Trent. It is a place of great antiquity, formerly of considerable importance.

The origin of the name Stafford has given learned antiquarians much trouble and remains in considerable doubt. Plott says,"About the year 705, the place or island where the town of Stafford now stands, anciently called Bethnei, began to be

STAFFORD FROM THE GRAND JUNCTION RAILWAY

inhabited by St. Bertelline, the son of a king of this country, and scholar to St. Guthlae, with whom he tarried until his death. After this, though now unknown to his father, he begged this island of him, where he led a hermit's life for years until he was disturbed by some that envied his happiness. He then removed himself to some desert, mountainous place where he ended his life. He left Bethnei to others who and called it Stafford, there being a shallow ford in the river that could easily be passed with only the help of a staff." Camden, copying the Saxon Chronicles, says, "Stafford was formerly called Betheny and was built in 913 by Ethelfleda, the heroic widow of Ethelred Earl of Mercia, and was a chief town in this country during the succession of the Mercian Kings. Ethelfleda also built a castle in the town for the protection of its inhabitants against the predatory incursions of the Danes from the northern part of England."

As no vestiges of the castle remain, the precise site on which it stood is unknown. The town was previously surrounded by a wall, fosse and had three gates, two of which give their names to two of the principal streets: Greengate and Gaolgate. In 1050, during time of Edward the Confessor, the Royal Mint was here, and pennies were coined in the town bearing the impressions of Edward and William the Conquerer with the words "GODWINNE ON STAEF" on the reverse. This denoted that they were struck by Godwinne, the King's moneyer, in Stafford. The word "on" Saxon language signifies "in", and Staef, a contraction of Stafford, was the spelling of the town's name then in use.

The place suffered greatly during the Civil War. Stafford gives titles to two peers of the realm, Lord Stafford, formerly Sir Jerningham; and Marquis of Stafford, now Duke of Sutherland, one of the Gower family. Perhaps no title has undergone more changes than that of the Barony of Stafford. It has been lost several times, and the present Baron obtained it by the reversal of the attainder of Sir William Howard, first Viscount Stafford, who was put to death in relation to his part in the Gunpowder Plot. In 1824, George IV restored Sir Jerningham, the descendant of the Viscount, to the Barony.

In 1575, Queen Elizabeth visited Stafford on her tour through England and restored the county court which had been removed to Lichfield. It appears that Stafford was incorporated before the time of King John, but the inhabitants first received a regular charter during his reign, confirming all privileges previously enjoyed. It was dated one year prior to that of London, and seven years before the signing of Magna Carta. Until the time of James I, the corporation consisted only of magistrates, and some time the chief magistrates or bailiff was a very low and improper person. In the seventh year of James's reign there was a petition presented by the most respectable members of the population for a mayor, aldermen, and capital magistrates, or common council. This corporation was forfeited in 1826 by the common council neglecting to fill up vacancies in the body corporate and, on petition, a new charter was granted by George IV in 1827. The borough has sent two members to Parliament ever since the reign of Edward I. Since the passing of the Reform Bill, the electors have been about 1180 in number. The population is about 9000.

There are two churches in the town, St. Mary's and St. Chad's. St Mary's is a large and ancient cruciform Gothic building, with an octagon tower rising from the middle and a Saxon parapet, consisting of a nave, two side aisles, a transept and a spacious chancel of three aisles. This church was formerly Collegiate, its architecture in the early pointed style, and although the windows, pillars, and arches are not alike in their order they are all very fine. The altar piece is an elegant example of workmanship of the Corinthian order, painted to imitate marble. The organ is considered one of the finest in the kingdom. The font is a curious piece of antiquity of very large and clumsy construction, having being carved out of a massive block of stone, and decorated with figures of men and animals. There are a number of ancient monuments in different parts of the church, most of which are very fine mural tablets. The most conspicuous, and indeed the only, altar tomb honors Lady Ann Aston and her husband, Lord Edward of Tixall. The living is a discharged rectory in the gift of the crown, but not a very valuable one; in the time of Elizabeth it was not sufficiently endowed to induce anybody to attend to the performance of the worship. "Not enough pay-not much prayers" was the motto.

The present rector has voluntarily added two services; one on Sunday evening, and one on Wednesday evening, so there are now three services on the Sunday, and one on the Wednesday. The other church, St. Chad's, is an older structure than St. Mary's. It is built to imitate of the earliest Saxon plan which assigned one half of the design to the nave, a quarter to the tower, and the other to the chancel. It was cased with brick about a century ago, and is therefore totally obscured. Its bells were sold to pay for repairs.

The Dean and Chapter of Lichfield draw away the revenues that belong to the church; the living is a perpetual curacy. In the parish of St. Mary's is an endowed chapel, the living of which is also a perpetual curacy. There is a small but handsome Catholic chapel, with a good house for the priest; a Presbyterian chapel; a large Methodist chapel; a New Connexion Methodist chapel; an Independent chapel; and a Quaker meeting house. All the churches and chapels have Sunday Schools connected with them, and thus, in some way or other, a little education is provided for the poorer classes. There is also a Grammar School, a National School, and an Infant School.

The Free Grammar School is endowed with an income of £335 and 13 shillings, of which two thirds is paid to the headmaster and the remainder to the usher, both of whom are appointed by the corporation but are subject to the approval of the bishop of the diocese. The school is open to all the boys of the town. The National School is endowed with £30 a year and, by means of both subscriptions and small payments from the children, 240 boys and 160 girls are educated. The Infant School was established by Mr Philip Seckerson.

There is neither a public library nor a philosophical institution. A Mechanics' Institute, however, has been established recently. One newspaper, the Staffordshire Advertiser, is around 40 years old, is published weekly and has a large circulation. The theatre may be mentioned as having had Mrs Siddons and the Duchess of St. Albans on its board before they became popular.

The charities consist of almshouses for poor aged persons, the Institution for the Relief of Widows and Orphans of the Clergy of Staffordshire, and the County Hospital, a most valuable institution where medical and surgical relief is afforded to the county's poor.

The almshouses are endowed with £50 per annum and there are other benefactions for the poor amounting in all to upwards of £120 a year, of which sum the celebrated Izaak Walton, the poetic angler who was born here, left about £90.

There is also a noble lunatic asylum, conducted on enlightened and philosophical principles. The building stands on an eminence in the midst of beautiful gardens which are cultivated by the unfortunate inmates. No nobleman's pleasure grounds could be kept in better repair, nor could any palace be in better order or more properly managed. It is most liberally supported by the neighbouring nobility and gentry, and possesses a fund for the assistance of those in troubling circumstances regardless of class, so each patient can associate with his own type and derive the greatest amount of benefit in the efforts to restore him to health and society. The expense of the institution is about £5000 per annum. From 1818, the year in which it was established, to 1837, about 1000 persons have been cured and nearly as many relieved.

The County Gaol is a large and substantial building where the criminal offenders are lodged. The House of Correction, which is attached to the gaol, is for the punishment of convicted offenders. There are eight treadmills, which are applied to the useful purposes of pumping water and grinding corn, along with a fulling mill. The annual expenditure is about £7000, although in 1799 it was only £843. The governor earns £450 per annum, and the chaplain £230.

The County Hall is a fine building in the centre of the High Street occupying nearly the whole of one side of a spacious square. It is 120 feet in length, ornamented with finely sculptured figures of Justice and Peace, and contains several handsome apartments. An assembly room stands in the centre, elegantly appointed and occupying nearly the whole of the length of the front. On each side are the court rooms for assizes and sessions, approached by a central staircase, at the top of which are the Grand Jury room and other apartments. The corporation

contributed £1050 to its construction. Stafford contains some good streets which are well paved, and the houses are generally well built. The inhabitants are supplied with plenty of good water. The entrance to the town from the London Road is via a neat bridge over the river, near one of the ancient gates.

The principal branch of manufacture is that of shoes which supply the London market and are also exported. Stafford has long been celebrated for its good ale.

There is a market every Saturday, when the town is well supplied with corn, meat, vegetables, butter, eggs, poultry, and so on. There are also annual fairs on the Tuesday before Shrove Tuesday and on the following days; April 3rd, May 7th and 14th for horses and cattle; the Saturday before St. Peter's Day (June 29) for wool; September 23rd for cattle and horses; October 2nd for colts; and December 4th for cattle and swine. The principal fairs are those in May, October and December. Races are held annually in September on Marston Field.

Stafford Castle is in the parish of Castle Church, a mile to the west of the town, once one of the finest Saxon fortresses. It is situated on a lofty, well-wooded eminence, exceedingly steep on the south side, and scarcely accessible. The castle was originally built by William the Conqueror, but after undergoing reversal of fortune and war, it was ultimately reduced to ruin and until around the end of the late war, when the late Sir Jernyngham restored a part of it to its original state. He cleared away the rubbish down to the first story, then made the platform clear for rebuilding. In removing the ruins many silver coins, mostly of a later date than Edward VI, a silver cross and a cannon ball were found, which of course now form a part of the castle's curiosities. The present Lord Stafford raised the south front and the two octagonal towers to the proper height, and made them of proper strength and thickness. Preparations have been made to rebuild the rest of the castle, but nothing further has been done since 1815.

We pass up the grounds through the outer gates and, ascending 30 steps, arrive at the base. The entrance accessed via two small doors in the towers

STAFFORD CASTLE

which lead into the hall, where there are many pieces of ancient armour and old furniture. Above is the armoury itself where complete suits of mail can be seen, along with lances, spears, and other weapons of baronial and knightly warfare. There are also some very curious relics of antique sculpture, most of them scripture pieces. In the rooms on each side of the towers are fine old pictures of the tournament and masquerade at Kenilworth in honour of Queen Elizabeth that celebrated Royal entertainment, which lasted 40 days and cost £1000 a day. In the room overhead are the remains of the tapestry of the former building, which contains some pieces of exquisite work in fine preservation. The scene of the crucifixion is most admirably portrayed. There is a fine carved oak bedstead, nearly four centuries old and which was used when the castle was in its glory, and some chairs, the backs of which were worked by the mother of the late Sir Jernyngham. From the top of the castle, 150 miles of the surrounding country can be seen. The Wrekin, in Shropshire, the Clent and Malvern Hills, in Worcestershire, the Vale of the Trent, leading to Nottinghamshire and the whole of the country around Stafford are visible. Our Saxon ancestors must have enjoyed the scenery

of the kingdom, for their castles were always on high hills and mostly by the side of rivers.

Not far from the castle is the village of Castle Church, a pleasant, rural place. Its church- an old but pretty building of Gothic architecture - stands in the midst of a neat churchyard a little way from the side of the road.

The countryside between Stafford and Lichfield is crowded with seats of the nobility and gentry, some of which we have already mentioned. About a mile beyond Shugborough is Ingestre Park, the seat of Earl Talbot. After passing down a couple of miles of winding carriage road through a noble sweep of park adorned with stately trees, from the tops of which cawing rooks proclaim the approach to some old English mansion, we at length see the hall. It is a fine old building in the Elizabethan style of architecture, partly hidden by fir and beech trees that form a dark background to the light and tasteful, though ancient, building. It is situated at the summit of a lawn, a vale immediately in front, in an immense extent of rising grounds, swelling wider and wider in the distance and adorned with all the beauties of sylvan scenery. At the south extremity of the valley, between the lawn and the park, is an

Stafford Castle

On crumbling knoll overlooking Stafford
The Norman castle, relic from the past;
Witness to how history's dice were cast,
Defeat of the Saxons with fire and sword.
Built in the classic motte and bailey style,
Dominating the area for miles,
The victorious Normans were the lords.

Recorded for all, in the Doomsday Book,
Saxons crushed after the Norman Conquest;
Stone castle built to thwart any unrest
And siege warfare when the King was unstuck.
Those Terrible Tudors, Duke lost his head,
War of the Roses, battlefields ran red,
Tudor politics and just plain bad luck.

English Civil War and fierce fighting,
Stafford Castle, a Royalist stronghold.
Defended by Lady Isobel, bold,
A staunch Catholic loyal to her King.
Cromwell won but the Castle was destroyed
By the demolition crews he employed.
A war is not "civil" - its suffering!

Just fortified trenches grown over green,
The remains of the Castle on the hill;
Its acres of earthworks were slowly filled,
Medieval deer parks no longer seen.
Castle and grounds became a sad ruin
And over which its stonework was strewn,
Butchered by masons with their crowbars keen.

If monuments could cry, then it would weep
And rebuilt in the 19th century.
Victorians wanted their history,
Restored as a Gothic Revival Keep.
Original stonework and foundations,
Stafford Castle, preserved for the nation,
Observing history in silent sleep.

Stafford Castle, symbol of passing years,
The motte and bailey gracing rising ground,
Hushed but for the swallows, with windswept sound
And the performance of plays by Shakespeare.
Children's laughter buries sadness and pain,
New life coming to the Castle again,
As the sun shines and shadows disappear.

INGESTRE PARK

elegant summer house overshadowed by beautiful trees, and in the midst of the park is a small octagonal building with the appearance of a temple of the woods. Hundreds of deer adorn the ground by day, and towards evening hares may be seen in great numbers. Much of the land is of the richest kind as it is near the banks of the Trent and its many tributary fertilizing rills, giving health to the soil. As a large proportion of the estate is cultivated by the noble owner, the appearance of the fields and meadows, with their fences and gates, is far above that of ordinary farming.

The house is in excellent condition and is magnificently furnished. The entrance is under a lofty tower, surmounted by a fine stone balustrade, from which rises a handsome observatory. There are a great number of good paintings and everything is calculated to impress us with the grandeur of nobility. The gardens, stables and farmyard are extensive and the farmhouse and labourers' cottages are all built in a style to harmonize with the hall; every house genteel, comfortable and neat. The eldest son of the Earl, Lord Ingestre, is one of the members for the Southern division of Staffordshire.

Near this seat is Western Farm, where there is a very productive brine spring and extensive salt work, at which 250 tons of salt are manufactured per week. These are a source of considerable revenue to Lord Talbot.

Passing by Weston, we come to Chartley, the former residence of Earl Ferrers. The mansion was destroyed by fire in 1781, and only a small gentleman's house remains which his lordship occasionally visits. There is a fine old park, containing 1000 acres of land and seems to be left to itself, or to the care of cattle and game. Chartley Castle is the ruin of an ancient Saxon fortress built in 1220 by Blundeville, Earl of Chester. The round tower is one of the largest and finest in the kingdom, the remaining portion appearing likely to survive another 1000 years. The hill on which the castle stands is very steep and lofty, and the spacious moat remains to this day scarcely filled, its sides covered with trees, most of which are fine old yews. The ivy, which has wound itself around the ruin, lends it a grace even in decay and holds it firmly together. The yews, while they appear as perpetual mourners, form a strong guard on every side, offering protection from wintry storms.

We move on to Sandon Park, the residence of the Right Hon. Earl of Harrowby, one of the speakers in the House of Lords. The park is very high from the

Woodland Lullabies at Ingestre Park

We pass down miles of winding carriage road,
Through pasture land and noble sweep of park;
Home to leaping hares and warbling larks,
Wildfire at the station, carriage our mode:
To Ingestre Park, our night time abode.
Stately trees adorn, from which rooks proclaim
"Visitors approach"!, their sylvan domain,
Haunt of graceful deer and pond-loving toads.

The Hall, a temple in a masquerade,
It's a Gothic style of architecture,
In excellent condition and structure,
Entrance surmounted by stone balustrade.
Twilight hues fall, intermixed light and shade,
The Hall hid by woods in a dark background.
The setting sun bathes the Park all around,
The artisans packing away their trades.

Hundreds of deer adorn the grounds by day,
Manufacturing district far behind;
Much of the land is of the richest kind,
River Trent fertilizing on its way.
We could not witness this from the railway,
The rills where the Trent's tributaries flow;
We came by carriage, lullabies by crows
And watched furtive rabbits come out to play.

Evening falls over this sylvan retreat,
The River Trent giving health to the soil.
Gentleman farmers, their backs bent in toil,
Now heading for home, their day's work complete.
Ingestre Park, a tasteful stately seat,
Is sleeping amongst the dells of the woods.
Labourers resting in the neighbourhood,
All is genteel, comfortable and neat.

road, and in front - at the top of the hill - is a lofty monument to the memory of Pitt, its head rearing above the highest of the stately trees that surround it. Passing through the gates and ascending the steep, winding road, we soon arrive at the Hall. It is an elegant, modern building composed of a centre with a handsome portico on Doric pillars and two light wings. The house is surrounded with delightful, cultured grounds, and in front is a spacious esplanade and lawn which leads down to the village church. It is bounded by a most beautiful series of lofty wooded hills and deep dark dells to the eastand is skirted with thickets and groves, giving the most romantic appearance to the scenery until it reaches the Trent.

Deep down in the valley flows the silver stream passing by mansions and villas and winding through the most Arcadian scenes that poet can wish for. The deer and game abound here as larks, thrushes and blackbirds trill their eloquent and powerful cadences. The spangled trout leap up from the surface of the water to enjoy the sunshine and feast upon the dancing flies, the pheasants and partridges flit about the hedges, the hares spring over the hills and the deer bound from glade to glade, all enjoying their existence and giving life and beauty to the scene.

From Stafford Station the road passes through a flat part of the country, the castle remaining in

...ASTLE

sight fo...
the righ...
some i...
of the ...
Mr Per...
marshy...
here. T...
small ...
of Sei...
Franci...
above...
the S...
of pea...
and a...
Statio...
Eccle...
Bridg...
little ...
Br...
seat, with its delightful flower g...
stream on the same side, is the next object. It was
formerly a convent, and if meditation and prayer were
the preoccupations of its residents, its situation must
have been highly favourable for such a state of mind.
A little further on are the silk mills of J. Milner and
his residence, Worston Hall. To the left of the line is

dell, close to the roadside, leading to some villages
nd hamlets with cottages for those employed in the
ills. The village of Worston lies over the hill to the
ight, and Chebsey, a part of Lord Lichfield's estate, is
o the left. The river is crossed here by a good stone
bridge of three arches. To the left, at a distance of
three miles, is Ranton Abbey, where Lord Lichfield
has a shooting and hunting box. There are enough
of the ruins of the abbey left to give picturesqueness
to the view; the lofty tower, the outward wall of the
church, and some of the cloisters remaining in a fine
state of time-hallowed preservation.

We now descend an inclined plane of half a mile
and arrive at the beautiful and romantic valley of
Shallow Ford. At this place two inclined planes of
the road meet and, as the river passes in an oblique
direction underneath and the ground is low on both
sides, no road could be made either under or over
the line, yet one was required. A constantly manned
small station-box is therefore placed here to give a
signal to the trains when anything is passing so that
they may moderate their speed.

This is one of the most delightful spots on the
road. To the left is a lovely "Vale of Tempe" where the
poet or painter may spend a day most delightfully.
On the west side of the vale is a range of steep

Lament for Chartley Castle

Chartley Castle was a Saxon fortress
And it was gutted and destroyed by fire:
As we pass, the Castle looks in distress,
Wounded by age because time never tires.
The tower, once the finest in the Kingdom:
Change comes and the works of men are undone.

Can it survive another thousand years?
The hill on which the Castle stands is steep;
The proud relic of ancient Staffordshire,
The remains of the motte and bailey keep.
Man made structures decay and fail to last,
The earth smothers structures whose time has passed.

The Castle ramparts are covered with vines,
The tendrils of ivy and fine old yews;
Green fingers around the ruin entwined,
Lending to it a grace for all to view.
Chartley Castle stands, even in decay,
A Saxon legacy alive today.

The yews are a guard for the departed,
Standing in protection from winter storms.
If human, they would be broken hearted,
Perpetual mourners of broken form.
Change is never-ending, without reason,
Only the earth renews through the seasons.

All things pass, we must go back to the earth
Like starlings cascading dusk into night;
A wave which rises and crashes like surf,
A waterfall of birds, seen at twilight.
All form and matter released, blowing free,
All but a stitch in time`s great tapestry.

Green tentacles, as if by some kraken,
Pull into a subterranean lair;
Transformed into wildflowers and bracken
The old workings of men, their labours bare.
As if in some answered prayer, the earth sighs:
Nought is eternal but the roaming skies.

The great works of men are out of the door,
As if humanity was never there;
Orchids carpet a sylvan woodland floor,
Trees blossom, midges dance in summer air.
A kingdom returning to the god Pan:
Bluebells, like the sea, gone the work of man.

Arcadian god Pan - he of the green,
Reclaims the earth, wildflowers are his crown;
The earth laughs in flowers, his glory seen,
Green sap flows and woodland leaves are his gown,
A woodland heaven, all around birdsong,
Where the god of our ancestors belonged.

wooded hills overhanging the stream. To the east is a lofty bank, covered with trees and shrubs, moss and heath, on the other side of which is the line of railroad, hidden from sight by the foliage and the winding course of the hills. The vale is a sequestered and shaded serpentine sweep of meadow, through which the river gracefully flows.

The side of the hill that rises from the river's margin is thickly covered with underwood, and stately trees hang their branches over spots of rich, evergreen pasture. Nothing is seen or heard to disturb the calm serenity of this peaceful valley, which is musical with the lowing of oxen and the warbling of birds, save the short and hurried rushing of the train, which is tracked only by its cloud of vapour.

The station-box is placed opposite the opening to this valley and close-by its side a road crosses the line from the east to the left bank of the stream, where there is an ancient farmhouse. To the right, a little wooden bridge over the ford leads to the village, which is situated amongst clusters of trees and adorned with gardens in which flowers for all seasons are tastefully cultivated. The hamlet is so peacefully serene that its sweet influence must be felt by those who happily live there. We can imagine it to be a remnant of a golden age. This is a famous angling place, and no doubt lzaak Walton hooked many a trout at Shallowford. Further on to the right is a flat, rushy swamp where the river takes a most curious serpentine course. We are now at Norton Bridge Station.

Shallowford - The Vale of Temp
(Staffordshire, God's Own County)

In England's heart, a woodland masquerade,
Where spangled trout leap to enjoy sunshine;
It's Staffordshire, footprints of the divine
And graceful deer abound from glade to glade.
All is peaceful, colours from light to shade,
Life and beauty to Staffordshire's county;
Tranquil and serene, from God this bounty,
A modern Garden of Eden portrayed.

Stags with antlers a yard and a half high
Roam like pheasants and partridge in hedgerows;
A land where the River Trent gently flows,
Joined to Heaven by hovering mayflies,
All is calm beneath peaceful summer skies.
Wild birds sing their eloquent cadences,
On silver streams the dragonfly dances,
Caught upon the breath of a poet's sigh.

Larks pour out matins, thrush and blackbird trill,
Each trying to outmatch their feathered tribe.
Wine of summer the avians imbibed,
Boarded by a series of wooded hills.
The River Trent irrigates with its rills,
A country scene - deer and game abound here,
This paradise, this unspoilt Staffordshire,
Mapped out with stately homes and water mills.

Enjoy existence, give life to this scene,
Carpeted with spangles of wild flowers,
Where noble trees rise like ancient towers,
Balm for the soul in the bounteous green.
Explore and see where God's footprints have been,
Green domains imprinted where they belonged;
To deny that God was here would be wrong:
Staffordshire is God's own country serene.

The road to Stone and Eccleshall crosses the line at the station, and there are omnibuses that attend the trains to take passengers to these places, both of which are about three miles off. Stone is a market town situated on the Trent and is the centre of an extensive parish, containing upwards of 7,000 inhabitants. It is the principal posting place between Stafford and Newcastle. The town is of great antiquity, having formerly had both a monastery and convent. The Saxon King of Mercia, Wulfere, who murdered his sons Ulfred and Rufin for becoming Christians, built a monastery in memory of them here. The population is employed in the manufacture of boots and shoes. A short distance hence, on the east side of the town, is Stone Park, the property of Lord Granville, a branch of the Gower family.

Eccleshall is famous as the residence of the Bishop of the Diocese. It is a very ancient place, having been occupied by the Romans and, as tradition has it, once had a temple to Jove on the site of the present Church. Eccleshall Castle, the residence of the bishop, retains nothing of its former fortified condition. In the year 1200, in the reign of King John, the bishop found it necessary to make redoubts and battlements, and to surround them with moats to protect his position.

The castle has gone to seed with the fall of the feudal system, and the present bishop lives in a comfortable and easily accessible modern mansion, which has a pleasant lawn and park. The late bishop Ryder was the brother of the Earl of Harrowby and the present bishop is Dr. Butler, for many years headmaster of Shrewsbury School. The bishop is the lord of the manor, and the sale of the wood of the estate brings in a considerable income.

The River Sow still accompanies us, and we cross it again by an iron bridge. To the right is the little village of Coldmeece, with a few pretty farm houses, and still further on is the hamlet of Yarnfield. On the left is the village of Badnall. Here, the line is level for a considerable distance and runs through fine open country. On the summit of the hill to the east we see Swinnerton Park and Hall, the seat of T. Fitzherbert, the son of the celebrated Mrs Fitzherbert, who was married to George IV when he was regent. A fine lawn, a mile in length and studded with magnificent trees, leads up to the Hall, a large and noble square stone building. On the north side is the parish church, with a square tower surrounded by thick foliage. The proximity of the parish church to the hall is a vivid reminder

SWINNERTON PARK AND HALL

of the times when it was established and supported chiefly by the aristocracy. The village of Swinnerton is a pretty little romantic and scattered place, abounding with rural walks.

We now come to Millmeece, another village where there is a large dam supplied by the River Sow, the stream from which turns a powerful flour mill. Here there is a strong and extensive bridge over the railway and the stream carrying the road from Meece to Swinnerton and Eccleshall. The line is exceedingly straight for upwards of two miles. To the left are the villages of Standon and Bowers, and to the right that of Cranberry. The view of the church and parsonage-house of Standon forms one of the most beautiful aspects on the whole line. The River Sow again flows under the road, and after we have passed over an embankment of half a mile in length, we come to Hatton Flour Mill, with its fine sheet of water.

On the hill to the east we see Trentham Coppice, a part of Trentham Park, and after passing through a cutting of about half a mile, the tower of Chapel Chorlton Church is seen to the left. This place is surrounded by hills rising in every direction, affording beautiful vistas of light and shade. The river winds along and the numerous farmhouses scattered over this part of the countryside give it a very enlivening appearance. Again we cross the Sow, and to the left is a romantic hill, completely enclosed by trees. We now pass through a cutting of sandstone upwards of 40 feet deep and come to a bed of peat more than 300 yards long and as black as coal. We enter another cutting of sandstone, in one place 60 feet deep where the rock rises perpendicular to the height of upwards of 40 feet. We then arrive at Whitmore Station.

This station is situated in a deep cutting of sandstone in the midst of a dark, wild and romantic heath, with hills and woods and some fine forest scenery. Gorse and broom are found in abundance, darkening the ground and spreading a sombre shade around. The road to Drayton, to the left, is a pleasant, sandy track through the dark line of hills surrounding it, and the opposite road to Newcastle runs through the beautifully rural

village of Whitmore, the seat and estate of Captain Mainwaring.

At a distance on the Drayton Road, the peaks of the hills, with their undulating surfaces and dark, shadowy drapery, lend the scenery magnificent character. About five miles to the east of the station is Newcastle-Under-Lyme, the road to which is extremely hilly and abounds with interesting views. By the side of the road there are many neat and elegant dwellings, and the land is well cultivated.

Newcastle-Under-Lyme is a market town and ancient borough. It derives its name from a new castle built in 1180 by Ranulph, Earl of Chester, replacing the old and decayed one at Chesterton, and the forest of Lyne, or Lyme, added to the name to distinguish it from Newcastle-upon-Tyne. It is situated on the road from Stafford to Manchester, and before the establishment of the railway a great number of coaches passed through daily. There is now only one. The population is between 8000 and 9000. It has sent two members to Parliament since the time of Edward III, and at the passing of the Reform Bill this privilege was continued, and the number of voters increased to about 950, of which 819 are freemen. The corporation consists of the mayor, two bailiffs, and 24 capital burgesses. There is a Court of Record, for the recovery of debts to the amount of £50. The principal employment of the inhabitants is hat making, along with some silk and cotton spinning.

There are two churches. The old parish church is dedicated to St. Giles the Abbot and is a dark-looking brick building with an ancient tower built of red sandstone. The living is a rectory, in the gift of the executors of the late, celebrated C. Simeon of Cambridge. The new church, St. George's, is a modern Gothic stone building, which cost £8000, towards which the late Rev. C. Simeon gave £1000, the corporation £500 and the inhabitants £500, raised by subscription. There is a very handsome and singular-looking Roman Catholic Chapel, built of brick in ornamental Gothic, which was designed and executed under the direction of the priest who officiates, the Rev. James Lynn. The altar window is a beautiful piece of stained glasswork. There are also a Wesleyan Methodist chapel, a new Connexion Methodist, an Independent, a Baptist, a Primitive Methodist, and a Unitarian chapel.

The Guild Hall, which is situated in the marketplace, is a large and handsome brick building supported by pillars, under which is the market hall. Above is an elegant cupola containing two clock dials that are lighted by gas. The gas works here are valuable, and the canals extremely serviceable, but unprofitable. There is a great deal of coal in the neighbourhood. A market is held on Monday for corn, and one on Saturday for provisions. There are five fairs in the year, a wake or feast, and horse races are held around the middle of July.

There is a Free School, with an endowment of £90 a year, an English School, with an income of £165, a Lancastrian school, a National School, and Sunday schools at every place of worship. There are almshouses for 20 widows, who each receive 3s a week, 4s at Christmas.

To the south of Newcastle-Under-Lyme is Trentham Park, the seat of the Duke of Sutherland. The road runs by the beautiful Trent Vale, through which the river meanders, the hills on each side crowned with woods. We pass the pretty village of

Handford and proceed alongside the vale, where the stream is occasionally overhung with willows and the lofty banks with hazels. Passing two small waterfalls, which are used to turn corn mills, we arrive at the village of Trentham, where there is a handsome inn opposite the entrance to the hall.

At a distance we see two towers, one old and the other new, and a confused mass of building, with a fine sweep of park to the right. On entering the gates, we pass by the stables and farmyard, and before us is the churchyard, surrounded by a magnificent row of horsechestnut trees, and along one side of which flows the river. The church is a fine Gothic building with a square tower, in good repair, and joins the hall by a passage through which the family accesses the church when they attend services. The pulpit cushion and cloth were once the saddle-cloth of the Emperor of Morocco. They consist of rich velvet, superbly worked with silver, and were formerly studded with diamonds and other precious stones. The saddle and bridle belonging to this cloth are kept in the saddle-house, and both are as richly worked in gold and silver as the cloth. There are many chains and other ornaments about them of the finest solid

TRENTHAM HALL

gold; even the stirrup slippers are covered with the precious metal.

The hall was formerly a heavy, square building without ornament, but of late considerable improvements have been made. A stately entrance, in the form of a crescent, has been added to its east front, with state rooms to one side and an excellent conservatory to the other. A spacious esplanade has been erected in front of the south entrance, with a marble terrace rising to the house. A new wing has been added to the west end, with a noble arcade reaching to the shrubbery and river, and from the centre rises a handsome Venetian tower. A large pleasure ground is being laid out at the south front, leading to a noble lake of 90 acres. To the left is the shrubbery, through which the river flows, and to the right is a majestic sweep of park rising to a lofty height and crowned with wood, with a colossal monument and statue of the late Duke in the centre.

As the Duchess of Sutherland holds the high office of Mistress of the Robes to her Majesty, it may be anticipated that this place will be graced with the presence of royalty. If rooms, with doors and panels rivalling ivory in appearance; with walls adorned with plate glass set in deep gold and beautiful paintings; with floors covered with the richest carpets and the most superb furniture; and views of the most romantic and delightful nature be any inducements for a Royal visit, there is certainly every luxury in which a Queen could indulge.

The hill on which the statue is placed is exceedingly lofty, and affords a fine view of the pool and its islands, the pleasure grounds, shrubberies, gardens, and hall. From this place, which is five miles from the railroad, the trains may be heard passing very distinctly when the wind is in the right direction. The statue of the late Duke was made by Chantrey and paid for by the tenants of the estate. An old soldier lives close by as a watchman over it.

The Duke, when at home, keeps up the old English - or rather Saxon - custom of giving bread and beer to any and everyone who may choose to take it. The almonry, near the church, has had sometimes as many as 500 visitors a day partaking in bread and beer. The cellars, of course, are commensurate with the scale of such hospitality. The Duke and his family are among the wealthiest of the nobility. The Duke is probably the greatest landowner in the kingdom and his brother, Lord Francis Egerton, inherits the Bridgewater estate, one made valuable by its canals and other works of art.

Leaving Trentham Park we now take time to visit the towns and villages that make up the other great manufacturing district of Staffordshire – The Potteries. This area is an extensive cluster of towns and villages more than ten miles in length and comprising six principal towns and 20 villages or hamlets. They contain a larger population, a greater proportion of good houses, more factories and wealth, more intelligent and ingenious people, more churches and chapels and schools, and probably more civilized and religious persons, than any other area of similar size. There is certainly much drunkenness and immorality, but by no means as much as in a cotton or woolen, or coal and iron districts. Both the continents of Europe and America obtain both luxurious and humble porcelain and earthenware for the table. It is simply the pottery of the world. No ancient pottery, however important, ever attained similar fame; wherever beer and tea are to be obtained, there are the jugs and cups of the Staffordshire Potteries. From the burning rocks of the Cape of Good Hope in Africa, to the icy cliffs of Greenland; from the Indian Sea, to the untraced regions of Australia, and round by the South Sea Islands to the Atlantic Ocean through the continent of America -wherever civilization makes its way, the plate, the dish, the tea cup, and the jug are found. Everything which is useful or ornamental for every meal, for prince or peasant, may be obtained here, from the simple milk basin to the elegant flower pot or ornamental vase; from the plain blue tea-cup to the transparent crystal and gilt tea service; from the common white plate to the elegant dessert dish.

In our visit to The Potteries we first proceed to Lane End and Longton. These towns are large and busy, containing from 9,000 to 10,000 inhabitants, and have risen over the last 60 years to their present condition from that of humble and obscure villages. They possess many large factories of earthenware,

VIEW OF THE POTTERIES FROM ETVIEVIA SOUTH, NEWCASTLE ROAD 1830

VIEW OF THE POTTERIES FROM BASFORD 1838

Explanations

Boundary of Proposed Borough   Red
Boundaries of Parishes or Townships   Brown
Rivers.   Blue

Robt R Dawson
Lieut R.E.

Scale 2 Inches to 1 Mile

R. Cartwright, Lith° Printer, Warwick Pl.

REFORM ACT PLAN OF THE BOROUGH OF STOKE ON TRENT 1832

REFORM ACT PLAN OF THE BOROUGH OF STOKE ON TRENT 1832

Sonnet to The Potteries

Earthenware, porcelain and luxuries
Across the world and untraced foreign ground;
The plate, dish, tea cup and the jug are found
And come from the Staffordshire Potteries.
Europe, America, Indian Seas;
From the frozen icy cliffs of Greenland,
Cape of Good Hope to the South Sea Islands,
Maker of jugs and cups for beer and tea.

Wherever culture makes its weary way,
The Potteries` genius is unfurled;
Staffordshire is pottery to the world,
Everything useful, here on display:
Simple vase to gilt tea service on tray.
No ancient pottery acquired this name,
No potters have ever won global fame:
The 6 towns of The Potteries portrayed.

porcelain and china that furnish employment to the inhabitants. There are many good houses and shops, two excellent inns, a spacious market hall, and a library.

There is a large Church at Longton, which cost £10,000, and a smaller one at Lane End, which cost £3,000. The Old Connexion Methodists have built two chapels, the New Connexion have also built two, the Independents have one, and the Catholics one. All these places of worship are exceedingly well attended and nearly all the children of the mechanics attend the Sunday Schools connected with them.

Stoke-upon-Trent is situated on the banks of the Trent, and though it is an important place in The Potteries, on account of being centrally located, it is the smallest and least important in terms of business and population. It contains some large factories and good houses, and the parochial business of the district is transacted here. The Potteries are grouped under one borough, that of "Stoke-upon-Trent". The town itself does not contain more than 5000 or 6000 inhabitants, but including the adjoining villages the population amounts to about 10,000.

The borough contains a population of upwards of 40,000, and sends two members to Parliament. The parish church was erected by contributions from the monarch down to the working man, at an expense of £14,000. The contributions are so curious that they should be noted: His Majesty George IV £250; the late rector, Dr. J. C. Woodhouse, £3,300 and £700 for an altar window; John Tomlinson, solicitor, and Josiah Spode, £300 each; J. T. Wheldon, £120; J. Smith, £100; the Society for Building New Churches, £400; the working classes, £500;£641 from Government as a remission of duty on the materials employed; £391 remitted dues from the Trent and Mersey Navigation Company; and £500 by team work from the inhabitants. The remainder was raised by rates. The living is a rectory, but by an Act of Parliament both its income and patronage are divided.

There are five chapels; a Wesleyan Methodist, two New Connexion, a Primitive Methodist, an Independent, and a Quaker meeting house. There is a large National School for the education of 500 children, which is liberally supported. The late Rector, Dr. Woodhouse, left £3,000 to support the National Schools of the parish. All the places of worship support Sunday Schools, of which the number amounts to nearly 50, and these afford religious education to upwards of 13,000 children.

Hanley and Shelton, though two distinct towns, now form one densely populated and well-built market town, containing several good streets, many handsome buildings, and extensive factories. The population is 16,338, of which 7,121 are in Hanley and 9,267 in Shelton, which includes Etruria and part of Cobridge. Hanley is the most modern, as well as the most handsome, town in the district. There is a good market hall, with a market every Wednesday and Saturday, the annual rent of the tolls being £1235. It is supplied with water by John Smith's water works, who has taken great interest in having a complete supply for the population. The gas works, near Etruria, were established in 1826 at a cost of £35,000 and supply the whole of The Potteries. There are two gasometers, each capable of holding 30,000 feet of gas, and the main pipes pass through 18 miles of ground.

There is a large brick church with a lofty tower in Hanley, which cost £5,000, and a large and handsome church at Shelton, built of stone in the early English style of architecture and which cost £10,000. There are nine chapels; two Wesleyan Methodists, two New Connexion Methodists, one Primitive Methodist, one Baptist, two Independent, and one Unitarian. A National School was erected in Hanley in 1816 under Dr. Bell's system, and a British School under Lancaster's. There are Sunday Schools connected with every church and chapel.

The Potteries Savings' Bank was established in 1823 and holds deposits of £30,000. There is a very excellent Mechanics' Institute, established in 1825, and a subscription library and news room. The district bank is a very handsome building of white brick in the Gothic style. The North Staffordshire Infirmary, founded here, is a large, substantial and plain edifice, capable of containing 100 patients. It is supported by subscriptions and endowments, and an attempt is being made to raise a permanent fund of £20,000 for its support. Altogether this is the largest and most important place in Staffordshire, and has

risen to its present condition from the manufacture of the district.

Burslem is the next town in importance. The most northern of those in this district, it may be said to be the mother of The Potteries, the first specimens of the area's craft having been manufactured here. It is a well built and advantageously situated place and, with its adjacent villages, contains 12,000 inhabitants. There are many good buildings and extensive factories. The manufacture of earthenware and porcelain is extensive here, and there are also factories producing glass, conducted by Messrs. Davenports at Longport. It was here that the great national undertaking, the Trent and Mersey Canal, was commenced by the celebrated Josiah Wedgwood. The district abounds with coal, ironstone, and clay; the strata of coal being found in the shape of a horseshoe. As many of the strata have been found at the surface, coal has been obtained in many places by what is called open work. Clay is used for the manufacture of bricks and pans for baking the earthenware and porcelain, and the coal mines yield an abundant supply of the mineral of which so much is required in the district.

In the centre of the market-place stands the large town hall where public meetings are held. The Market days are Monday and Saturday, and there are six fairs held over the course of the year. The town is governed by a chief constable. Water and gas are supplied from Shelton and Hanley. There are some subscription warm baths, which are very useful.

A large and handsome Parish Church was erected in 1828 at a cost of £12,000, nearly the whole of which was a grant from government, and a Chapel-of-ease is being erected at Sneyd Green. There is a Catholic chapel, and seven other places of worship; two of the Old Connexion Methodists, two of the New, one of the Primitive Methodist, one Baptist, and one Independent. There is a Free School, a National School, and Sunday Schools connected with each place of worship. There are other places worthy of special notice in this district, but the observations in this work are necessarily limited.

After our visit to The Potteries we leave Whitmore Station to continue our journey northwards, with

BURSLEM-BELL-WORKS

BURSLEM-BLACK-WORKS

the village of Whitmore to the east of the railway line. It is a pleasant little place, situated in a romantic and sequestered valley, its ancient Church and rustic turret peeping through the surrounding trees, giving a beautiful effect to the scene. Whitmore Hall is a handsome old English building situated at the bottom of a deep and rocky dell through which a little stream finds its way. The sides of the hills around are covered with dark wood and shady plantations. The owner is Capt. Mainwairing, who earned for himself an honourable distinction in the British navy under the command of Nelson and deserves to be recorded among the benefactors of the human race

for rescuing persons from death by fire and water.

Keele Hall, on the same side, is a handsome house standing on a lofty eminence overlooking a delightful valley, covered with wood and shrubs. It is the residence of Ralph Sneyd, a large coal and iron master.

On leaving the station, we pass through a considerable bed of peat which is nearly as black as coal. The origin of its formation is little understood, but it is an extremely valuable substance being extensively used for fuel. In Ireland, where coal is scarce and the population little employed, were it not for the peat beds most of the poor would have

BURSLEM CHURCHYARD WORKS

BURSLEM IVY HOUSE

KEELE HALL

no fire whatsoever. Peat grows only in wet or moist places, about two thirds of it is carbon and the rest earth and iron ore. On each side of the road, a considerable quantity of iron is deposited from the water which flows from the peat. Occasionally there are solid masses of iron ore found peat beds. While so much moisture is required for its production, it is generally found in hilly places where the ground is and spongy with water.

We next come to fine, open countryside of beautiful pasture land. On the left is Madeley Manor Farmhouse, backed with dark firs. A little further on in the same direction is another farmhouse, from which wreathing smoke ascends, by the side of a tree-covered hill. To the right a sparkling brook flows along the margin of some rich pasture land, and on the left we come to Hay House, a shooting box belonging to Lord Crew. We now have arrived at Madeley Station.

To the right, close to the roadside, are the remains of the grounds of Mr Weston Young, a gentleman of considerable fortune and spirit who used to keep a pack of harriers on his estate, one which was excellently preserved. He had an expensive lawsuit with the railroad company for spoiling his grounds, which he lost when it was proven that he had let part of them for a farm. To the top of the hill, on the right, we see some tall chimneys belonging to the works of Mr. Firmstone at Leysett Colliery, where as many as 20 different measures of coal are found, along with various beds of ironstone. The local district, from Silverdale to Apedale, abounds with minerals, and Mr. Firmstone is constructing a railroad to his works in order that he may run his own engines to supply the companies' stations with coke, and convey the iron to Birmingham and Manchester.

To the left is a high spot of wood called Barr Hill with a fine view of the surrounding countryside from the summit that reaches as far as Wales. The road is exceedingly straight here, and we can see for several miles along the line, under the bridges, which gives a beautiful perspective.

Great Madeley is a pretty village in the parish of Madeley. Containing about 1,000 inhabitants, the houses and cottages are built of stone, having the brook which runs by the side of the road passing through it and forming a dam, which turns a corn mill. There is a fine, cruciform old Gothic church that is dedicated to all saints and is in good repair, as if in a collegiate town. The interior is fitted very handsomely in oak, and there is a good organ but, unfortunately, no organist. The Earl of Wilton, who is one of the finest organists in the kingdom, is a large pew holder in the church and one of the Lords of the Manor. The Hon. Elizabeth Emma Cunliffe Offley, Lord Crewe's aunt, is the Lady of the Manor and lives at the manor house a little further on.

A miser by the name of Stretch, having fallen into a pit in the neighbourhood one dark night, gave himself up for lost but found his way to Madeley by the sound of a bell. He died eventually in 1804 from the consequences of his fall, but bequeathed a bell and salary for ringing it every night from eight to nine o'clock in his will so that others in similar circumstances might also find the road.

We now pass a deep cutting, of 50 or more feet in some places, through undulated hills between which we see beautiful vistas of the countryside, and soon come to an embankment from whence we have a view of a most romantic dell bounded by shadowy hills, abrupt precipices, and heathery banks. As far as we can see from the right, the vale stretches out in colourful beauty, bordered by a thick wood to the left.

We glide over another embankment 30 feet high, beneath which passes the stream that flows through the valley, and proceed through a cutting of gravel and sandstone in many places more than 30 feet deep. Very large sized granite boulders are occasionally found here. We then pass over a very long embankment some 40 feet high, from which we see the village of Wrinehill on the right, its hall and mill on the left. The millers in this neighbourhood complain that the engines rob them of water, so that in dry seasons they are unable to work. To the right is a deep valley, beautifully wooded, leading to Heighley Castle and Silverdale.

We next come to a cutting through Bunker's Hill. There is an opening to the right through which we see Betley, a picturesque little village in the valley a mile from the road, and Betley Court, a fine old English hall at the top of a rising lawn, skirted with wood, and bounded in front by a large sheet of water called Betley Mere. Still further to the right is Betley Hall, the residence of G. Tollet. One of the hills by the roadside affords a fine view of the country, which is delightfully varied with valleys, woodlands and pastures.

Wildfire has now crossed the borders of Staffordshire into the county of Cheshire, concluding our part of the journey through one of the most diverse and beautiful counties in the land. Staffordshire may often be overlooked in its status, yet it is a county rich in a history it is entwined with throughout many centuries of change. Its population continues to swell in and around the now vast manufacturing districts that were the spark for the Industrial Revolution, giving the growing towns a fresh scope of life and civic impetus. It is a region of understated importance, a designation that will surely be addressed in the fullness of time.

To the End of the Line

We now exit the borders of Staffordshire,
All on board our noble locomotive;
The Wildfire journeys on into Cheshire
As if we had a royal prerogative.
Train picks up speed, to borders palatine,
Forward on the Grand Junction Railway line.

Stay on board the Wildfire, please turn the page,
This rushing engine with sound of thunder.
For posterity, we record the age,
A changing world and scenes of great wonder;
All seen from the embankment with fine views,
Staffordshire under summer skies of blue.

Markets are passed with their cattle and swine
And labourers hard at work on their farms;
Staffordshire, witnessed from the railway line,
A rushing commotion, we cause alarm
And we are then gone, this clattering train:
Vapour behind and all is quiet again.

The train rushes at 40 miles per hour
And seems to fly down inclines at night;
The engine is driven by just steam power,
The Wildfire through Staffordshire is a sight.
Wildfire, a marvel of machinery,
Travelling on through Cheshire`s scenery.

It seems we have the wind`s velocity,
The acme of pure mechanical force;
All this from steam, power in purity,
An expansion of water, nature`s laws.
We rush along and it seems that we glide,
Bound for Cheshire, on the Wildfire, we ride.

We are at a loss whom to admire most:
Inventions of man or laws of nature;
To whom salute and to whom should we toast?
Are there angels in the architecture?
Cheshire calls and we journey up the track:
Staffordshire behind, there`s no looking back.

ITINERARY OF THE JOURNEY 1838

Left to Liverpool.	Line of Railway.	Right to Liverpool.
	BIRMINGHAM Station.	
	Bridge over the Birmingham Canal. Embankment and Viaduct.	London Line branches off after passing this bridge.
	Embankment.	
Temporary Station.	Duddeston Bridge.	
	Cutting.	Duddeston Hall, formerly the seat of S. T. Galton, Esq.
	Embankment.	Old Castle Bromwich road.
	Short Cutting.	Saltley Chapel in the valley,—Mrs. Hallan's house on the further eminence.
Aston Park.	Aston Embankment.	Castle Bromwich, about 5 miles.
Aston Hall, with its avenue, the seat of James Watt, Esq.	Mill Pool.	Tame new channel.
		Artificial Pool.
	Viaduct over the Birmingham and Fazeley Canal.	Turnpike Road to Lichfield.
		Water Works and Reservoir.
	Aston Viaduct.	Farther on, Gravelly Hill and Erdington Slade.
Aston Village and Church.	Excavation, depth 24 feet.	Witton Hall.
		Oldford.
		Oscott College.
	Bridge.	Township Road from Birmingham to Aston.
The Village and Church of Handsworth.	Bridge.	New Turnpike Road from Birmingham to Walsall.

Left to Liverpool.	Line of Railway.	Right to Liverpool.
Farther on, Soho.	PERRY BARR Station, 3½ miles. Cutting. Cast-iron Bridge. Hampstead Cutting. Bridge. Embankment.	Perry Barr Hall, the seat of John Gough, Esq., with its Church and Rectory. Tame new Channel.
Hampstead Hall, the residence of T. L. Moilliett, Esq.		Turnpike Road from Birmingham to Walsall.
Farther on, Sandwell Hall and Park, the seat of the Earl of Dartmouth.	Shallow Cuttings and Embankments. Newton Excavation. Embankment. Cutting. Cross the Tame twice.	Mill Pool.
		Mill Pool.
Charlemont, the residence of Mr. Alford.	NEWTON Bridge and Station, 6½ miles. Gates. Embankment.	
Coal and Iron District of West Bromwich.		Road from Great Barr to West Bromwich crosses the Railway.
Birmingham and Staffordshire Gas Works.	Tame Cutting. Bridge.	Road from Walsall to West Bromwich.
Crown Glass Manufactory of Messrs. Chance, Brothers, and Co.	Shallow Embankments and Cuttings.	
Farther on, the Town of Dudley.	Bridge.	Turnpike Road from Walsall to Wednesbury.
Wednesbury.	BESCOT BRIDGE Station, 9½ miles. Cast-iron Bridge across the Tame. Bridge.	Bescot Hall, the residence of Mr. Marshall. Walsall. Walsall and Darlaston Turnpike Road.
	JAMES'S BRIDGE Station, 10½ miles. Bridge. Darlaston Green Cutting. Aqueduct.	Township Road from Darlaston to Bentley.
		Bentley Branch of the Birmingham Canal.
	Embankment. Bridge.	Township Road to Darlaston.
Darlaston.		Aqueduct of the Darlaston and Walsall Branch of the Birmingham Canal.
Farther on, Bilston.		

Left to Liverpool.	Line of Railway.	Right to Liverpool.
	Bridge. Willenhall Cutting. WILLENHALL STATION 12 miles. Bridge.	Road from Willenhall to Darlaston. Bentley Hall.
Road from Bilston	Shallow Cutting.	To Willenhall.
Road to Wolverhampton.	Four occupation Crossings. Bridge.	From Walsall.
	Wednesfield Excavation.	Wednesfield Village.
Wyrley and Road from Wolverhampton	Bridge. Tunnel, length 186 yards.	Essington Canal. To Wednesfield.
Wolverhampton.	WOLVERHAMP-TON STATION. 14 miles.	
Road to Wolverhampton Oxley Hall.	Embankment. Bridge. Shallow Cuttings and Embankments.	From Cannock.
Road to Wolverhampton Wrottesley Hall.	Bridge. Six Bridges. Iron Bridge across Staffordshire and Worcestershire Canal. Embankment.	From Bushbury. Bushbury Church and Hall Moseley Hall. Moseley Court. Farther to the right, Hilton Hall.
Chillington Hall. Somerford Hall. Brewood.	Four Bridges. FOUR ASHES Station, 19¾ miles. Two Bridges.	
Old Watling Street	Bridge.	Roman Road.
	SPREAD EAGLE Station, 21¼ miles.	
Road from Wolverhampton	Bridge. Excavation. Cutting.	To Stafford.
	Two Bridges. Embankment.	Teddesley Hall, Lord Hatherton. Beyond, Cannock Chase.
	PENKRIDGE STATION, 23¾ miles. Two Bridges.	Penkridge.

Left to Liverpool.	Line of Railway.	Right to Liverpool.
	Viaduct.	River Penk.
	Cutting.	Village of Acton Trussell.
	Embankment.	Farther on, Shugborough Park, Earl of Lichfield.
	Excavation.	Tixall Hamlet.
	Bridge.	To Stafford.
Road from Wolverhampton	Slight Excavations and Embankments.	Ingestrie Hall, Earl Talbot.
Road from Wolverhampton	Bridge.	to Stafford.
Road from Newport	Bridge.	to Stafford.
Stafford Castle.		
	STAFFORD	Stafford.
	Station, 29¼ miles.	
Castle Church Village.		Chartley Castle, Earl Ferrers.
	Cutting.	
	Two Bridges.	Sandon Park, Earl Harrowby.
	Shallow Embankment.	
	Bridge across Doxy Brook.	
	Excavation.	
	Bridge.	
	Embankment.	Great Bridgeford.
Seighford Hall, Francis Eld, Esq.	BRIDGEFORD STATION, 32½ miles.	Bradford Hall.
Road from Eccleshall	Bridge.	To Stafford.
	Cutting.	
Road from Worston	Bridge.	To Stafford.
	Embankment.	
	Three Bridges over River Sow.	
	Shallow Cuttings and Embankments.	
	Shallowford Village.	
	Norton Cutting, 15 to 20 feet deep.	
Road from Eccleshall	Bridge.	To Stone.
Eccleshall.		Stone.
	NORTON BRIDGE Station, 34¾ miles.	
	Embankment.	
	Bridge over River Sow.	
	Cutting.	
	Bridge over the Sow.	
	Shallow Embankment and Excavation.	
	Mill Meese, (Village)	

Left to Liverpool.	Line of Railway.	Right to Liverpool.
Road from Eccleshall	Bridge.	To Swinnerton.
Road from Eccleshall	Bridge.	To Newcastle.
	Bridge over River Sow.	
Sow new Channel.	Embankment.	
Standon Village.	Bridge over River Sow.	Swinnerton Hall, J. Fitzherbert, Esq.
	Hatton Cutting.	Swinnerton Church.
Road from Woore	Bridge.	To Stone.
	Whitmore Cutting.	
Road from Market Drayton	Bridge.	To Newcastle.
	WHITMORE Station, 43 miles.	
Market Drayton.		Whitmore Village.
	Shallow Excavation.	Farther to the right, the Staffordshire Potteries.
	Madeley Station, $45\frac{3}{4}$ miles.	Leysett Colliery, Mr. Firmstone.
	Excavation.	Madeley.
	Bridge.	
	Bridge.	
	Embankment.	
Road from Woore	Bridge.	To Newcastle.
	Short Cuttings and Embankments.	
	Excavation through Bunker's Hill.	Betley Village.
	Three Bridges.	Betley Court.
	Embankment.	
	Basford Intermediate Station.	Crewe Hall, Lord Crewe.
	Short Cuttings and Embankments.	
Road from Nantwich	Three Bridges.	To Sandbach.
Nantwich.	**CREWE STATION,** $53\frac{3}{4}$ miles.	
	Embankments and Cuttings.	
	Bridges.	
	Coppenhall Station, 55 miles.	
	Embankment.	
	Minshull Vernon Station. $58\frac{1}{2}$ miles.	

Left to Liverpool.	Line of Railway.	Right to Liverpool.
Middlewich Branch	Cutting. Bridge. Embankment. Bridge. Cutting. Bridges. WINSFORD STATION, 61 miles.	Canal.
In the distance, Beeston Castle. Winsford Village. Wharton Village.		Middlewich.
Cross the River Weaver. Vale Royal Abbey. Farther on, Delamere Forest. Road from Chester	Cuttings. Bridges. Vale Royal Viaduct. Embankment. Hartford Cutting. Two Bridges.	Bostock Hall, J. France, Esq. To Northwich.
	HARTFORD Station, 65¼ miles.	Hartford Village. Northwich.
Grange Hall, Lady Brooke.	Short Cutting and Embankment. ACTON STATION, 68 miles.	Farther on, Marston Salt Works. Weaverham Village.
	Excavation. Two Bridges. Embankment. Cross Dutton Wood. Embankment. Dutton Viaduct. Cross the River Weaver and Navigation Canal. Cutting. Embankment. Cross Bird's Wood. Excavation.	Acton Village. Course of the Weaver.
Road from Runcorn	Preston Brook Cutting. Tunnel (100 yards.)	To Northwich.
Road to Chester	Bridge. PRESTON BROOK Station, 72¼ miles.	From Warrington. Junction of the Trent and Mersey, and the Duke of Bridgewater's Canal.
Duke of Bridgewater's	Aqueduct.	Canal.
Norton Priory, Sir R. Brooke. Farther to the left, Runcorn.	Embankment. Moore Cutting Four Bridges.	Daresbury Firs. The Elms.

Left to Liverpool.	*Line of Railway.*	*Right to Liverpool.*
	MOORE STATION, 74¾ miles. Bridge. Embankment. Warrington Viaduct. Cross the Irwell and Mersey Canal, and River Mersey. Arpley Embankment. Three Bridges.	Latchford.
	WARRINGTON Station, 77¾ miles.	
Road from Liverpool Course of the Sankey Canal.	Bridge. Bradley Embankment WINWICK STATION. NEWTON JUNCTION Station, 82½ miles.	To Manchester. Spire of St. Paul's Church The Bone Works. Halford Hall. Winwick Village.
Chemical Works.		The Vulcan Foundry.
Burton Wood. Sankey Canal	Enter upon the Manchester and Liverpool Railway. Sankey Embankment. Sankey Viaduct. COLLIN'S GREEN Station.	Newton Race Course. Crosses the Railway.
Bold Hall and Park.	Cross Parr Moss. ST. HELEN'S JUNCTION Station. Iron Bridge.	Parr Village.
St. Helen's and Runcorn Gap Railway.	Excavation. LEA GREEN STATION. Rainhill Level. KENDRICK'S CROSS Station.	Sutton Hamlet. Shirley Hall.
	Rainhill Bridge. Sandstone Cutting. Whiston Embankment. HUYTON GATE Station.	Prescott. The Hazels. Farther to the right, Knowsley Park, Earl of Derby. Huyton Village.
Childwall Hall. Summer Hill House. Nutting Ash Church. Broad Green Village.	ROBY LANE STATION. Broad Green Embankment. BROAD GREEN Station.	Wharf for the Embarkation of Cattle.

Left to Liverpool.	Line of Railway.	Right to Liverpool.
Two lines of Rails, leading to the Company's Warehouses at Wapping.	Olive Mount Cutting, (70 feet in depth). WAVERTREE LANE. EDGE HILL STATION. Tunnel under the town of Liverpool. LIME STREET Station.	

Left to Manchester.	JOURNEY FROM NEWTON JUNCTION TO MANCHESTER.	Right to Manchester.
	NEWTON JUNCTION Station. Sandymain Embankment.	
Turnpike Road from Wigan Newton.		To Warrington. Winwick.
Farther on, Haydock Park The Leigh Arms. County Club Room.	NEWTON BRIDGE Station, 16 miles from Liverpool. Embankment. Viaduct.	In the distance, the Staffordshire Hills. Hotel and Post Office.
Road from Newton		To Warrington.
Wigan Junction Railway.	PARK SIDE STATION. Kenyon Excavation.	Slab in wall, commemorating the death of Mr. Huskisson.
Bolton and Leigh Railway.	BOLTON JUNCTION Station. Brossley Embankment.	Culcheth Hall and Township.
	BURY LANE STATION. Embankment. Cross Chat Moss.	
Astley Village. Farther to the left, Tyldesley Village.	LAMB'S COTTAGE Station. BARTON MOSS Station.	
Worsley Hall.	PATRICROFT STATION. ECCLES STATION. WEASTE LANE Station. Bridge over the Irwell. Manchester.	Eccles, the Village to which Mr. Huskisson was conveyed from Park Side. Trafford Hall.

STATIONS OF THE GRAND JUNCTION RAILWAY AND LIVERPOOL TO MANCHESTER RAILWAY

BIRMINGHAM STATION OF THE GRAND JUNCTION RAILWAY

Distance to Liverpool or Manchester, 97¼ miles.

Vauxhall Station.

Distance to Birmingham, 1½—Liverpool and Manchester, 94 miles.

Perry Barr Station.

Distance to Birmingham, 3½—Liverpool and Manchester, 94 miles.

Newton Road Station.

Distance to Birmingham, 6¾—Liverpool and Manchester, 90¾ miles.

Bescot Bridge Station.

Distance to Birmingham, 9½—Liverpool and Manchester, 88 miles.

James's Bridge Station.

Distance to Birmingham, 10¼—Liverpool and Manchester, 87¼ miles.

Willenhall Station.

Distance to Birmingham, 12—Liverpool and Manchester, 85½ miles.

WOLVERHAMPTON STATION.

Distance to Birmingham, 14¼—Liverpool and Manchester, 83¼ miles.

Four Ashes Station.

Distance to Birmingham, 20—Liverpool and Manchester, 77½ miles.

Spread Eagle Station.

Distance to Birmingham, 21½—Liverpool and Manchester, 76 miles.

Penkridge Station.

Distance to Birmingham, 24—Liverpool and Manchester, 73½ miles.

STAFFORD STATION.

Distance to Birmingham, 29¼—Liverpool and Manchester, 68¼ miles.

Bridgeford Station.

Distance to Birmingham, 32¾—Liverpool and Manchester, 64¾ miles.

Norton Bridge Station.

Distance to Birmingham, 35—Liverpool and Manchester, 62½ miles.

WHITMORE STATION.

Distance to Birmingham, 43¼—Liverpool and Manchester, 54¼ miles.

Madeley Station.

Distance to Birmingham, 46—Liverpool and Manchester, 51½ miles.

Basford Station.

Distance to Birmingham, 52—Liverpool and Manchester, 45½ miles.

CREWE STATION.

Distance to Birmingham, 54—Liverpool and Manchester, 43½ miles.

Coppenhall Station.

Distance to Birmingham, 56—Liverpool and Manchester, 41½ miles.

Minshull Vernon Station.

Distance to Birmingham, 58¾—Liverpool and Manchester, 38¾ miles.

Winsford Station.

Distance to Birmingham, 61¼—Liverpool and Manchester, 36¼ miles.

HARTFORD STATION.

Distance to Birmingham, 65¾—Liverpool and Manchester, 31¾ miles.

Acton Station.

Distance to Birmingham, 68¼—Liverpool and Manchester, 29¼ miles.

Preston Brook Station.

Distance to Birmingham, 72½—Liverpool and Manchester, 25 miles.

Moore Station.

Distance to Birmingham, 75—Liverpool and Manchester, 22½ miles.

WARRINGTON STATION.

Distance to Birmingham, 78—Liverpool and Manchester, 19½ miles.

Winwick Station.

Distance to Birmingham, 80½—Liverpool and Manchester, 38¾ miles.

Newton Junction Station

Distance to Birmingham, 82½—Liverpool and Manchester, 14¾ miles.

NEWTON JUNCTION TO LIVERPOOL

Fourteen and ¾ Miles

Collin's Green Station

St. Helen's Junction Station

Lea Green Station, (top of Sutton incline,)

Kendrick's Cross Station, Rainhill

Huyton Gate Station

Roby-lane Station

Broad Green Station

Wavetree Lane Station

Edge Hill Station

LIME STREET STATION LIVERPOOL

NEWTON JUNCTION TO MANCHESTER

Fourteen and ¾ Miles

Newton Bridge Station

Park Side Station

Bolton Junction Station

Bury Lane Station

Lambs Cottage Station

Barton Moss Station

Patricoft Station

West Lane Gate Station

Cross Lane Bridge Station

MANCHESTER STATION

REGULATIONS OF THE GRAND JUNCTION RAILWAY

TIME OF DEPARTURE.—The doors of the Booking Office are closed precisely at the time appointed for starting, after which no passenger can be admitted.

BOOKING.—There are no Booking Places, except at the Company's Offices at the respective Stations. Each Booking Ticket for the First Class Trains is numbered to correspond with the seat taken. The places by the mixed Trains are not numbered.

LUGGAGE.—Each Passenger's Luggage will, as far as practicable, be placed on the roof of the coach in which he has taken his place; carpet bags and small luggage may be placed underneath the seat opposite to that which the owner occupies. No charge for *bona fide* luggage belonging to the passenger under 100lb. weight; above that weight, a charge is made at the rate of 1d. per lb. for the whole distance. No kind of merchandise allowed to be taken as luggage. The attention of travellers is requested to the legal notice exhibited at the different stations, respecting the limitation of the Company's liabilities to the loss or damage of luggage. All passengers by Railway will do well to have their luggage distinctly marked with their names and destination.

GENTLEMEN'S CARRIAGES AND HORSES.—Gentlemen's carriages and horses must be at the Stations at least a quarter of an hour before the time of departure. A supply of trucks are kept at all the *principal* Stations on the line; but to prevent disappointment it is recommended that previous notice should be given, when practicable, at the Station where they may be required. No charge for landing or embarking carriages or horses on any part of the line.

ROAD STATIONS.—Passengers intending to join the Trains at any of the stopping places are desired to be in good time, as the train will leave each Station as soon as ready, without reference to the time stated in the tables, the main object being to perform the whole journey as expeditiously as possible. Passengers will be booked only conditionally upon there being room on the arrival of the Trains, and they will have the preference of seats in the order in which they are booked. No persons are booked after the arrival of the Train.—All persons are requested to get into and alight from the coaches invariably on the left side, as the only certain means of preventing accidents from Trains passing in an opposite direction.

CONDUCTORS, GUARDS, AND PORTERS.—Every Train is provided with Guards, and a Conductor, who is responsible for the order and regularity of the journey. The Company's Porters will load and unload the luggage, and put it into or upon any omnibus or other carriage at any of the Stations. No fees or gratuities allowed to be received by the Conductors, Guards, Porters, or other persons in the service of the Company.

SMOKING, SELLING OF LIQUORS, &c.—No smoking is allowed in the Station-houses, or in any of the coaches, even with the consent of the passengers. A substantial breakfast may be had at the Station-house at Birmingham, by parties, going by the early train; but no person is allowed to sell liquors or eatables of any kind upon the line.—The Company earnestly hope that the public will co-operate with them in enforcing this regulation, as it will be the means of removing a cause of delay, and will greatly diminish the chance of accident.

Goods sent to Birmingham, Manchester, or Liverpool, by the evening Trains, are generally delivered early on the following morning.

VISITING THE SOUTH STAFFORDSHIRE MINING AND MANUFACTURING DISTRICT 1838

During our journey we travelled through the mining and iron manufacturing district, now we shall make some observations on the general character of this part of the county of Staffordshire, and its people, in particular that of those occupied in the production of pig iron and coal mining.

If the operations of mining had not so disfigured it, the scenery of this part of the country would be most beautiful. The county consists of magnificent hills and delightful valleys, and is adorned with rich foliage and pasture; but in this southern extent, all these have been so spoiled by the working of the mines, that they are hardly ever thought of, and their effect never felt. Thousands of acres have been upturned, and the contents of solid rock and earth taken away, in many places to the thickness of 30 yards, at the depth of 200 yards or more. The hills have been excavated for the iron and limestone which they contained, and the valleys filled up with the refuse of coal, clay, slate and stone. Huge mounds of slag or cinder now form dark artificial hills that blend in to this blackened landscape.

The people instead of enjoying the variegated scenery of nature on the surface of the earth have been engaged in exploring its bowels by the dim light of the torch and candle. They have been working like Vulcans in the volcano, or wandering like ghosts in the regions of Hades.

They have blasted the bowels of the earth at midnight, making hideous thunder, for the ore – they have hewn out of the black and smoky carbon wherewith to melt it – they have put out the light of day by their caverns, and imitated it by night, with their enormous and terrible fires, blast furnaces burn furiously with regular deafening noise adding to the fervour. They have lived with danger and death till they have lost all fear of either; and they have been removed from civilization, until they have almost returned to barbarism. In the very heart of science, they remain utterly and hopelessly ignorant; supplying the world with wealth and luxury, ornament and grace, they are without many of the comforts of life, and are the most rugged in person, and unsightly in dress, that can be found in the kingdom. They are, however, kind and attentive to strangers, and, considering their occasional poverty, and the temptations to which they are consequently subject, remarkably honest.

The population of the mining and manufacturing district is upwards of 200,000, the greater proportion of whom are unable to read, and are so degraded in their ignorance, as not to care for their condition, or for that of their children. They have their enjoyments, it is true, and they perform very important services to mankind.

IRON WORKS AND THE SMELTING OF IRON

Across the manufacturing district Iron Works are working around the clock, day and night, their blast furnaces constantly in action smelting iron from the ore that abounds in the region, along with the other materials required in the process.

The smelting furnaces require, for many hours, the application of the most intense heat, in order to separate the pure metal from the substances with which it is by nature combined. For this purpose the ironstone is mixed with charcoal, and a furious power of blast from an air piston, worked by a steam engine, is directed into the fire, on the ironstone

STAFFORDSHIRE COLLIERS

and charcoal or coke. The metallic part separates itself from the combination provided a sufficient quantity of a third substance is added, which has such a chemical affinity for the extraneous matter, as to cause a union of the two, in the form of a semi-vitreous fluid, which hardens in cooling, into a slag or cinder; while the iron, by its superior specific gravity falls to the bottom of the furnace in which the fusion is affected; and thence suffered to run off, comparatively free from impurities. This third substance, whatever it is, is called "flux". The Staffordshire iron ore, being of a kind called "argillaceous" and has a base of clay. The flux used in this case is limestone to liberate the iron. Limestone abounds in the Staffordshire district, lying under the strata of coal and iron ore, and in several places crops out or comes to the surface.

A Staffordshire furnace is usually about thirty feet square, - or, if circular, about the same measure in diameter, at the base; the dimensions at the upper part being a little more than half; and the height forty-five to fifty feet, exclusive of the turret. In its exterior, an iron furnace takes the general form of a truncated pyramid, or cone, surmounted by a cylindrical turret or chimney.

At the base are constructed arched entrances or recesses, one for the admission of the workmen who manage the furnace and draw off the iron, - and others for the introduction of large pipes communicating with the steam engine apparatus, and by means of which, powerful and equable blasts or streams of air are constantly driven upon the heated materials within.

From the drawings of one of the local ironworks, figure 1, a large portion of the building is solid masonry. The ground plan, figure 2, shows the entrances and position of the blast pipes, and figure 3 shows the form of the cavity destined for the reception of the iron ore and other materials. This cavity, in the different portions of its elevation, takes different names; the lower and smaller part, which receives the melting metal, is called the hearth, (A). This is of cubical form, and its sides are squares of about three feet each way. The capacious division next above, is called the boshes; it widens suddenly from the hearth, to (B); where it is fifteen or sixteen

Fig.1.

Fig.2.

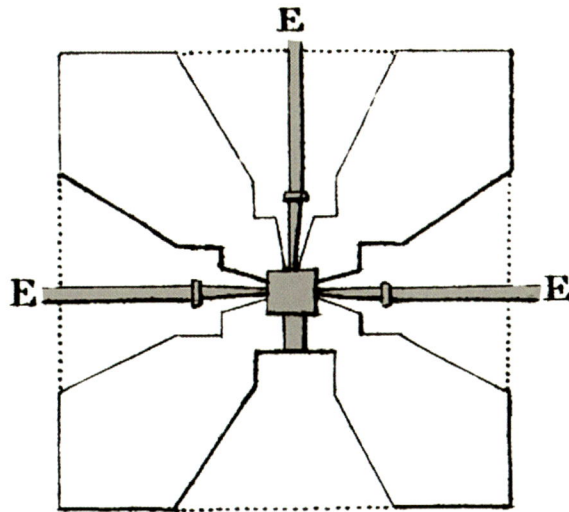

Fig.3.

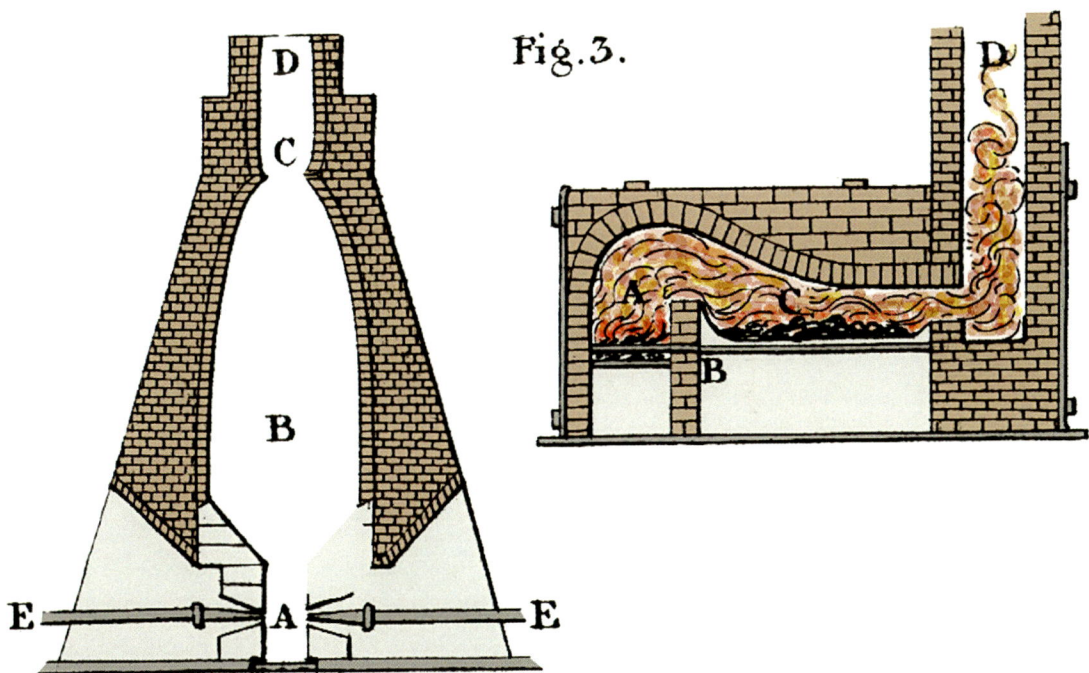

feet in diameter; and afterwards becomes gradually narrower, under the name of the tunnel, (C); until it terminates in the cylindrical turret, (D), called the tunnel head; in which latter are doors or openings, for the admission of the materials. The hearth, and the lower part of the boshes are lined with large blocks of coarse and very durable species of grit-stone, procured at Gornal, a village near Dudley. The pieces of this stone are joined and cemented together, with fire-clay. The upper part of the boshes, and the tunnel, are lined with fire bricks; and the strength of the whole is assisted by the use of strong hoops or bindings of iron.

The mode of admitting the blast will be gathered from the comparison of figure 2 and 3. The pipes are introduced into the hearth, through openings at a little distance from the ground. Their conical terminations are called "twyeres", vernacularly "tweers", and sometimes "tue-irons". Of these pipes, two, at least, are now usually introduced into each furnace, and in some cases three or even four in order to obtain the requisite amount of heat.

Adjacent to the furnace is placed a steam engine of such power and force adequate to supply the blasts, and to provide the additional motional power required for mechanical assistance. From the level area, at the summit of the furnace, descends an inclined plane of wood work, along which, up grooves, fixed for the purpose, move horizontal stages or platforms, on which are placed large barrows containing the iron ore, the lime-stone flux, and the coke as fuel. To raise these loaded platforms to the upper level, is part of the task of the steam engine; and in each transit, the ascent of the charged barrows is in some degree assisted by the descending weight of the empty ones. In a few favourable situations, advantage is taken of a sudden declivity, which is scarped out, and the precipitous front supported by masonry, close to which the furnaces are built; so that the materials are wheeled by the workmen, without mechanical aid, from the upper level of the ground to the top of the furnace. Near the town of Bilston we may also observe a furnace, fed by a series of buckets to a revolving

CASTING INGOTS   DRAWING THE CRUCIBLES

chain, similar to the action of a chain pump.

Witnessing the furnaces of manufacturing districts is not for the faint hearted, the roar from the blast pipes is heard from miles around, especially by night, when their uncaring fury is strikingly awful. Nor is the terror of them diminished, by approaching more closely. The power of blast which a forty-horse engine can produce from a piston containing many hundred cubic feet of air, and sometimes many thousand feet, is appalling to those who have never heard it before. No sound that we have previously heard gives us any feeling or notion which can be compared to it. At the proper time, the person who has the management of the work, having prepared the moulds of sand for the reception of the liquid metal, with an iron bar pushes a hole through at the bottom of the furnace, and the metal begins to flow. The stream of red and white hot metal iron pours forth in awful volume and dazzling light, and from the surface arise brilliant and beautiful flames of many colours, and most resplendent and glorious scintillations. Sparks, spangles, crosses, and stars of flame, shower up from the glowing surface, and make the most vivid and changing impressions

CASTING PIPES

on the eye. The stream of metal seems living with glory and beauty; changing its form and hue, but preserving its brilliancy. At length the metal begins to set, and the various degrees of oxidization which different parts have undergone, produce a great variety of colour, imitating the hues of the rainbow. The metal is allowed to cool, and in that state called pig iron.

Such is the iron furnace; in which, when once the fire is kindled, it is never suffered to become extinct, while the work is carried on, – being constantly fed by the perpetually recurring supplies of fuel being thrown in. When, from any cause, a furnace ceases working, the significant phrase used to express the circumstance, is, that it is "blown out".

Let us now experience some of their scenes underground, let us now visit a mine and descend a coal pit.

DESCENDING DOWN A COAL PIT 1838
Clothing ourselves for the occasion in suitable apparel, we get into a large iron basket and descend.

The sides of the pit appear to pass up quickly by us as we go down, and we alight at length on the floor of the mine, the bottom of the shaft. Here all is awful darkness, and every object is solid blackness. We can hear in the distance the sound of the collier's pick-axe; the crushing fall of coal, and voices which are human. After a few minutes, a candle is put into our hands, and we grope our way trying our best to keep up with our guide. We find there are many passages leading from the place where we alighted, roofed and pillared, with black, but sparkling coal. These massive pillars which support the roof of the passage may be one, two, or three hundred yards from the surface of the earth. We wander along, probably half a mile in one direction, amidst the strata, away from the only entrance to light and air, the dislocated rock over our heads and under our feet, and rows of pillars of coal on either hand. A horse suddenly emerges out of another passage, dragging after him a large and heavy load on a tram road, and accompanied by a young boy. Turning into the passage from whence he came, we soon arrive at

BOTTOM OF THE MINE SHAFT

the place where a group of miners are at work.

Let us see a bed of coal obtained. Beyond the pair of pillars that are beside us, we see a thick mass of coal: the miner seats himself on the ground, and with a pick-axe, undermines it, perhaps a yard in depth, three or four in breadth, and six or eight in length, taking care to leave sufficient supports at each of the four corners. The sides are then cut through in a similar manner, when the front of the bed is propped up with wood and coal, and the supports cut away. The prop being pushed down, the whole bed breaks off from the layer of coal which is next above, and falls, the weight of which is sometimes twenty or thirty tons. This piece is then broken up and carried away; another mass is obtained in the same manner, a pillar being left on each side, for the protection of the roof.

The height of the more lofty passages varies from ten or twenty yards to three feet, where we have to grope along, the candle being scarcely sufficient to light our way. The pillars are magnificent and wonderful, and strike us with more of the awfulness and terror of the sublime in architecture than anything which we see in the Gothic height of the cathedral roof.

Many are the passages through which we go, and in each of them we find men and boys naked to their waists, working the mine. There they are, covered with coal dust, and reeking with perspiration; their bright eyes glittering through their blackened faces, and the place around them just made "palpably obscure" by the feeble light of a few candles. At every strike the dust flies, and when a large piece of coal is obtained, such as we have described, the place contains, for some time, an atmosphere of coal. We therefore expect to partake of the hue of the surrounding air, and are prepared to give proof of the locality which we have been visiting.

STAFFORDSHIRE MINER WITH SAFETY LAMP

SOHO – WHERE GENIOUS AND THE ARTS PRESIDE EUROPA'S WONDER AND BRITANNIA'S PRIDE

About a mile from Birmingham and a small distance from the line of the Grand Junction Railway stand the very elegant and extensive Manufactory of Soho, belonging to the family of those two ingenious and scientific gentlemen, Messrs. Boulton & Watt. It is impossible to leave out a more detailed account of this great national manufactory; for its establishment, and the perfection to which the arts attained under the talents and enterprise of its great founder Matthew Boulton.

It is greatly to be lamented that, an improper use having been made by some foreigners, of the indulgence granted them in being admitted to see the manufactory, restrictions have been the consequence, and no part of the premises are now open for exhibition, except the elegant show room. However we can now reflect on the creation of this great Manufactory and the marvellous men of ingenuity and invention

THE STORY OF SOHO

Matthew Boulton was a native of Birmingham born on 3rd September, 1728, who established himself on Snow Hill as a manufacturer of "toys". It is said of him that he "would buy any man's brains", and in this lay his great secret of success. He did not expect perfection. He patiently trained people to do their work and was a keen judge of character. His pleasant manners, genial temper and unflinching justice made him honoured, loved and feared, an excellent manager of men.

Back in 1757, Handsworth Heath was a barren heath, occupied only by a rabbit warren, but in that year, John Wyrley, Lord of the Manor of Handsworth,

MATTHEW BOULTON

granted a lease for 99 years to Messrs. Rushton and Evans, with liberty to divert Hockley Brook and to form a pool for the requirements of a water mill for rolling metal. In 1761, the lease was purchased by Matthew Boulton who rebuilt and enlarged the mill, however it was too small, and in 1764, the foundations were laid for the great manufactory which became the scene of many noble triumphs. It was completed in 1765 and consisted of four squares, with connecting ranges of workshops, capable of accommodating a thousand workmen. He was joined by a Mr Fothergill and they established a design and manufacturing centre for vases, candelabra, tripods, and silver plated wares, which led to the establishment of an Assay Office in 1773.

Matthew Boulton's many projects led him to seek additional power to execute them as water power

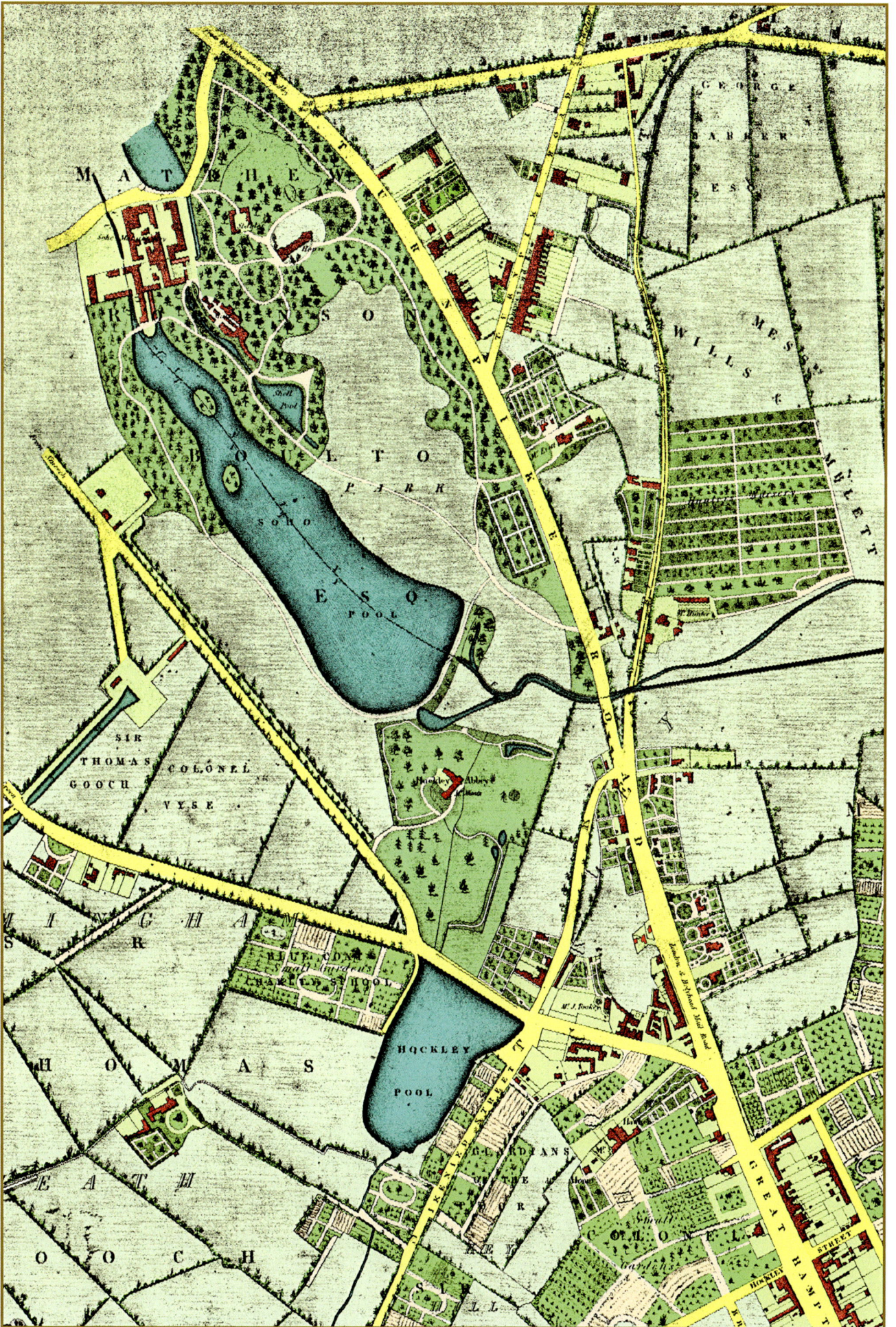

MAP SHOWING THE SOHO MANUFACTORY c1824

MATTHEW BOULTON'S SOHO MANUFACTORY 1800

was insufficient to suit his needs, and in 1767, he erected a steam engine, on the plan of Savery. He soon made the acquaintance of James Watt, a mechanic in Glasgow who had perfected valuable improvements in the steam engine. In 1775, Boulton & Watt entered into a 25-year partnership to build parts for, and to assemble Watt's engine at the Soho Manufactory. They charged a premium to customers who bought the engine, which amounted to one third of the saving in fuel made by their engine, compared with a common one. The engines created great interest, and enquiries and orders soon began to arrive at the Manufactory.

Among the many other manufactures to which the steam engine was found applicable was that of coining, for which a purpose built mill was erected in 1788. With the aid of a few boys, eight machines were worked, each capable of strking seventy to eighty four pieces a minute, the size of a guinie; which is equal to between 30,000 and 40,000 per hour; and at the same blow, which strikes the face and reverse, the edge of the piece is also struck, either plain or with an inscription. In 1797 Matthew Boulton was awarded the Royal Mint contract to strike copper coinage at Soho. Boulton's design was to produce a coin which should be "inimitable" but his coinage was imitated by lead pennies, faced with copper. To foil this, he made his twopenny pieces

exactly 2oz in weight, and eight of them measured a foot. The pennies weighed 1oz and seventeen measured two feet, and so on.

By this time Boulton & Watt steam engines Boulton & Watt steam engines and mining equipment were being exported worldwide. However, realizing that when the original patent expired in 1800, the payment of premiums would vanish, the partners saw that they would have to make and sell complete engines on a large scale if they were to continue in business. The Manufactory was unsuitable and the tools were inadequate, so they decided to build entirely new premises dedicated solely to engine construction. In 1795, Boulton & Watt bought the land for a foundry and, in a very short time, the necessary buildings were constructed. On January 30th 1796, the Soho Foundry was officially opened.

WILLIAM MURDOCH

Right from the very start of the Boutlon & Watt partnership back in 1775 in the manufacture of steam engines, one of the greatest difficulties experienced by the Soho firm was that of obtaining skilled workmen; another was that of keeping them when they had obtained them. The first difficulty they overcame by confining the men to special classes of work; carrying the division of labour to the farthest possible point; by Boulton to cope with it.

There were tempters from abroad continually lurking about Soho, offering heavy bribes to obtain access to the works; and still heavier to lure away skilled workmen. The "Waggon and Horses" Inn, at Handsworth, was a hot bed of temptation for gathering intelligence about the secrets of Soho. It was here that Pickard picked up the idea of the crank steam engine, and thus forestalled Watt in the use of that improvement.

Boulton was fortunate to meet with the one person who gave promise of becoming a thoroughly trustworthy workman and valuable helper – a young Scotsman, William Murdoch, who had travelled to England in search of employment.

William called at Soho in 1777, to ask for a job and he saw Boulton – work was slack with them at this time, and every position was filled. William nervously kept twirling his hat with his hands. It was not a felt hat, nor a cloth hat, but painted and composed of some unusual material. The hat was made of wood – William had turned it himself on a lathe. Boulton saw the young man with new interest and estimation – his wooden hat was proof that he was a mechanic of no mean skill, and he was asked to call again.

When he next called, he was put upon a trial job, which gained him a permanent situation, fifteen shillings per week. Murdoch soon proved himself worthy of confidence and was sent to Cornwall where many Boulton engines were at work in draining the mines, and had hitherto required the almost constant presence of James Watt.

When living in Cornwall as resident engineer, Murdoch turned his attention to the subject of the locomotive engine, and actually brought the idea to a certain degree of perfection – this later fell into oblivion until George Stevenson took it in hand, and carried the project to a successful issue.

When Murdoch returned to Soho, he was given the general supervision and management of the mechanical department, where he introduced several valuable improvements in the manufacture of the steam engine. But the invention by which his name will chiefly be remembered was that of lighting gas. The inflammable qualities of coal gas had long been known, but William Murdoch applied the knowledge to practical uses. He turned his attention to the subject and dreamed of the brilliant artificial light of the future. He put his discovery of the production of gas from coal to use, by lighting his house at Redruth, Cornwall, and then at the Soho Manufactory.

THE LUNAR SOCIETY

Matthew Boulton was a man of thoroughly social disposition, and made friends wherever he went. He was a favourite with children and philosophers. When at home, he took pleasure in gathering about him persons of kindred tastes and pursuits, in order at the same time to enjoy their society and to cultivate his nature through talking with minds of the lightest culture. He formed friendships with Benjamin Franklin, Dr Small, Dr Darwin, Josiah Wedgewood, Thomas Day, Lovell Edgeworth and others equally eminent, out of which grew the famous Lunar Society.

The members met once a month, by turns at each other's houses, always at full moon, in order that distant members might drive home by moonlight – hence the name of the society. At these meetings, the members exchanged views upon all subjects relating to literature, science and art. Here, Murdoch, Darwin and Lovell Edgeworth talked about their pet project of steam locomotion; here Dr Priestly told of his marvellous discoveries in chemistry, kindling an enthusiasm in the minds of Boulton & Watt for the study of science, which bore fruit in certain of the ingenious productions at Soho. It was a marvellous gathering of fine intellects. Absence from the meetings was always sorely lamented by the unfortunate "Lunatic" detained for whatever reasons.

Each member was at liberty to bring a friend with him and among the visitors thus introduced were Sir William Herschel, Sir Joseph Banks, De Luc, Dr Camper, Dr Solander, Dr Samuel Parr, Smeaton the engineer, and many other men of science. The Lunar Society continued to exist for many years from 1777, but one by one the members dropped off. Dr Priestly emigrated to America; Dr Withering, Josiah Wedgewood, and Dr Darwin died before the close of the 1700's, and without them, a meeting of the Lunar Society was no longer what it used to be.

WEST BROMWICH
TO DUDLEY AND THE
CASTLE AND CAVERN

At a small distance from the line at Newton Station is the village of West Bromwich, and just behind the market town of Dudley, with its historic Castle and subterranean mines. West Bromwich was until lately little more than a village; but from the working of the rich iron and coal veins which abound here, it has risen into a town of considerable importance. The meaning of the name is, a "village" on the "Broom" or Heath; "Brom" signifying Broom or Heath, and Wich, or Wic, a village or township. The term "West" was added, because it was situated to the west of the residence of the Lord of the Manor. It is, as might be expected, very irregularly built, but the main street contains some very good houses and a few handsome buildings, and is nearly a mile in length.

Among the various branches of manufacture, which are conducted on the most extensive scale, are guns and pistol barrels and locks, swords, bayonets, fire irons, fenders, hinges, nails, saddlers' ironmongery, coach furniture, iron culinary utensils, chains, traces, spades and other implements of husbandry, steel toys, gas tubes and fittings, palisades, and ornamental work of every kind. There are the furnaces for the smelting of iron ore, foundries, forges, and slitting mills, in all of which steam engines are employed.

The neighbourhood abounds with Coal Pits, and there is one lately sunk by Lord Dartmouth on the Heath, it has taken five years to reach a depth of 927 feet, where a bed of coal nine feet deep is to be found, steam engines equal to eighty horse power currently work it. The place around is extremely black and dirty, and the work people, in general, are as dirty as the place: they are rough, course, uncultivated and uneducated, and violent set of men, daring and reckless, but steady and ingenious in their own business.

We make our way now to the visible focal point of the castle on the hill in the distance, and the town of Dudley. It is a market town, standing on the boundary line in an isolated part of Worcestershire, with most of its population employed in the operations of mining, or of the manufacturing of iron or glass. The place is said by Camden to derive its name from "Dodo" or "Dudo", a saxon prince, to whom it belonged at the time of the Heptarchy, who built a castle here. The town is very dirty, from the neighbouring works, and always seems busy with employment.

The manufactures arise chiefly from the geological character of the neighbourhood, which is remarkable for the variety and extent of its mines of coal and ironstone, lying on each side of a line of basaltic rock and limestone. There are numerous coal pits in this neighbourhood, varying from a depth of 300 to 390 feet. Among the beds of coal, is one of excellent quality and great thickness, called the "Ten – yard Coal", below which another stratum, varying in thickness, has been discovered within the last twenty years. There is also raised from the same shaft what is called Heather Coal, from strata of smaller dimensions, at different depths from the surface. Immense mines of ironstone are also found between these veins of coal that not only afford an abundant supply of this useful material to the numerous works here, but are conveyed from hence by means of canals to several of the midland counties. There are also many smelting furnaces and several large flint glass manufactories.

116

DUDLEY CASTLE 1840

DUDLEY 1840

The men engaged in the working of the pits around Dudley, and in the smelting of iron, usually obtain high wages; and boys as young as ten years of age obtain good wages readily, so much is labour in demand in these parts. However, the manners of the working class locally are rude and rough, and but few signs of the schoolmasters magic march are seen. They are fond of good eating and drinking, and they usually get it; but are careless of personal appearance or household comfort.

The Castle. This is an interesting ruin of a once magnificent and strongly fortified place. The grounds around the Castle are beautifully laid out, which afford a great time to the lovers of cultivated and tasteful scenery. From the various parts of the road leading to the castle, we obtain different views of the country, which, were it not interrupted by the fire and smoke of the furnaces, would be extremely picturesque.

The castle consists of portions of two or three towers, and the remains of a spacious and splendid suit of apartments, built in a square form, and enclosing an area of a hundred yards across. The ruin stands on the top of a lofty hill, which was formerly inaccessible on every side except the south, where was the grand entrance. The hill was surrounded with a moat, over which was a drawbridge with two portcullises.

The Castle was encompassed with two thick walls, parts of which still remain. From the commanding situation of the towers, there is a noble view of more than fifty miles round the country. To the south, on one side, is seen the lofty dark range of the Malvern Hills, eight miles beyond Worcester; on another the Abberley and Clent Hills, and the Monument in Hagley Park, the seat of Lord Lyttleton. To the west, arise the Clee Hills, and the Wrekin, the lofty and celebrated mountain of Shropshire. To the north are situated the important mining and manufacturing districts of Tipton, Bilston, Wednesbury, West Bromwich, and Wolverhampton; and to the east lies Birmingham, in which six churches are visible.

Near the Castle is the Priory, a beautiful Gothic building, seated in a lovely valley, and surrounded with delightful shrubbery walks, where the chief agent of the estate resides. A little further, in the same direction, is the Wren's Nest Hill, a limestone quarry; which has a very remarkably appearance when the sun shines brightly. Another hill, about half a mile south east, is the spot from which Oliver Cromwell, in 1644, besieged the Castle. The first Dudley Castle was built during the Saxon Heptarchy, as early as the year 700. It was demolished in the time of Henry the Second, re-built in the reign of Henry the Third , much injured in the civil war between Charles and his Parliament, and ultimately destroyed by fire in the year 1750. The place is the property of Lord Ward.

The Cavern, however is the most remarkable object of attention. Almost the whole of the extensive and lofty hill on which the Castle stands is undermined and excavated, for the purpose of obtaining the limestone, which is found there in great abundance. On the north side of the hill, there is a large opening, into which the visitor enters, and there he sees a magnificent and lofty line of gloomy subterranean arches, supported by vast and massive pillars, under which passes the canal, where boats are seen with beings moving about in them with dull lights in their hands, like unearthly spectres. Nothing gives so complete a notion of fabled regions of Tartarus and the melancholy stream of Styx, which is duly attended by a Charon. An immense region of gloom appears which may readily be imagined to be the dwellings of the dead, the awful and terrifying Hades. As the place becomes more familiar to the eye of the observer, he finds that the arches are all composed of the stratum or vein of the rock, and the pillars are but a portion of the different strata, left in that shape in the working.

The height of the arch is in many places forty of fifty yards, and the width is often as much: the whole of this place having been made by blasting and digging away the solid rock. We find that there are two or three subterranean passages containing water, even under our feet, forming canals from the transit of boats, which convey the stone away from the works , one of these is a mile and three quarters long, thirteen feet high, and nine feet high, and is, in some places more than twenty yards below the surface, forming a communication with the Birmingham and Stourbridge canals, another is not more than a quarter of a mile, through which the visitor will most probably pass to see the works. We get into the boat, and pass underground, experiencing a still more awful sensation than we felt on entering the cavern, as we must trusts ourselves to the skill and integrity of the miners and boatmen who seem to inhabit these regions in the bowels of the earth. By the light of dim candles, we witness the narrow and low dimensions of this canal, and cannot help feeling some of the horror which is so natural to humanity, on being shut up in a small boring in the midst of the earth, with water below us, and the solid eternal rock above us. Occasionally, we find relief from this impenetrable gloom, by coming to an opening in the cavern, where the dim pent passage is exchanged for the lofty and sublime, but terror-clad and shadowy arches and pillars again. As we move along, we hear at a distance the thunder of the blasting of the rock, reverberating terrifically through the cavern. At length we come to an opening wide and yawning, where two or three passages are perceived leading to various parts of the excavation and turning suddenly to the left, we soon find ourselves near the works, which is indicated by the appearance of the miners bringing the stone down to the boats. Quitting the boat, we proceed along a narrow low path to an open part of the cavern, and passing an ascent of the hill; and arrive at the works.

Here a large arch is being cut out, and men and boys are busily engaged with pickaxes, crow bars, and other mining tools, each one having a candle fixed in a lump of clay. The mode in which they work is this. They bore a hole into a piece of the rock, and placing a ramrod in the hole, put some powder in, and plug the ramrod in with soft stone, The ramrod is then withdrawn, and a straw filled with fine powder is put in its place. A bit of paper is then greased into the candle, and being attached to the straw, one end of the paper is lit, and the workmen retire to a distance, or behind part of the rock. The paper burns slowly to the straw, when the explosion instantly takes place. The burst and reverberation of the horrible din which is heard, is such as few persons have experienced before. Pieces of stone are sometimes hurled to a great distance with immense force; but as the miners always know the direction of the blast, an accident scarcely ever happens. We now ascend the steps before mentioned, and find ourselves on the verdant banks of the hill; scarcely can we help feeling regret, at last, to quit the regions which we have been exploring.

VIEW OF CREWE HALL ORIGINALLY PUBLISHED IN 1818

OSBORNE'S MAP OF THE GRAND JUNCTION RAILWAY – 1838

E dward Osborne, James Drake, Thomas Roscoe and James Wyld became well known for their early railway journals, in particular those produced for travellers on the newly opened Grand Junction Railway. They each produced their own menu of historical and topographical content in terms of the scenery, places and objects, on either side of the line, however none would be complete without an actual map of the railway route that could be referred to whilst undertaking the journey.

The same base map was used by all four visionaries, being very detailed and showing many of the places, stations and other features along the line, however each preferred their own choice of illustrations that appeared on the map itself. Drake's map showed a drawing of the locomotive Wildfire, with carriages and wagons. Osborne's map was illustrated with the "Centaur" again with carriages and wagons; back in the very early days of the Grand Junction Railway other engines ran the route such as Falcon, Lynx, Eagle, Surocco and Dragon.

The map that follows has been meticulously re-constructed in full colour from Osborne's original black and white map. This was folded into the 1838 guide and allowed the map and descriptive accounts of the many places on route to be used together by the early railway travellers. The numbers on the sectional map overlay on the next page spread refer to the corresponding page numbers that follow, each illustrating that section of the map in full detail.

RAILWAY BRIDGE NEAR PENKRIDGE WITH TEDDESLEY HALL IN THE DISTANCE

OSBORNES' MAP OF THE GRAND JUNCTION RAILWAY

INCLUDING THE

LIVERPOOL & MANCHESTER. RUNCORN GAP & St HELENS. NEWTON & WIGAN AND LEIGH & BOLTON LINES.

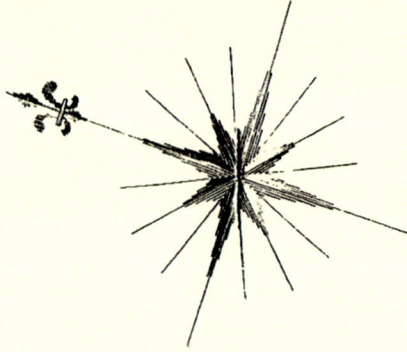

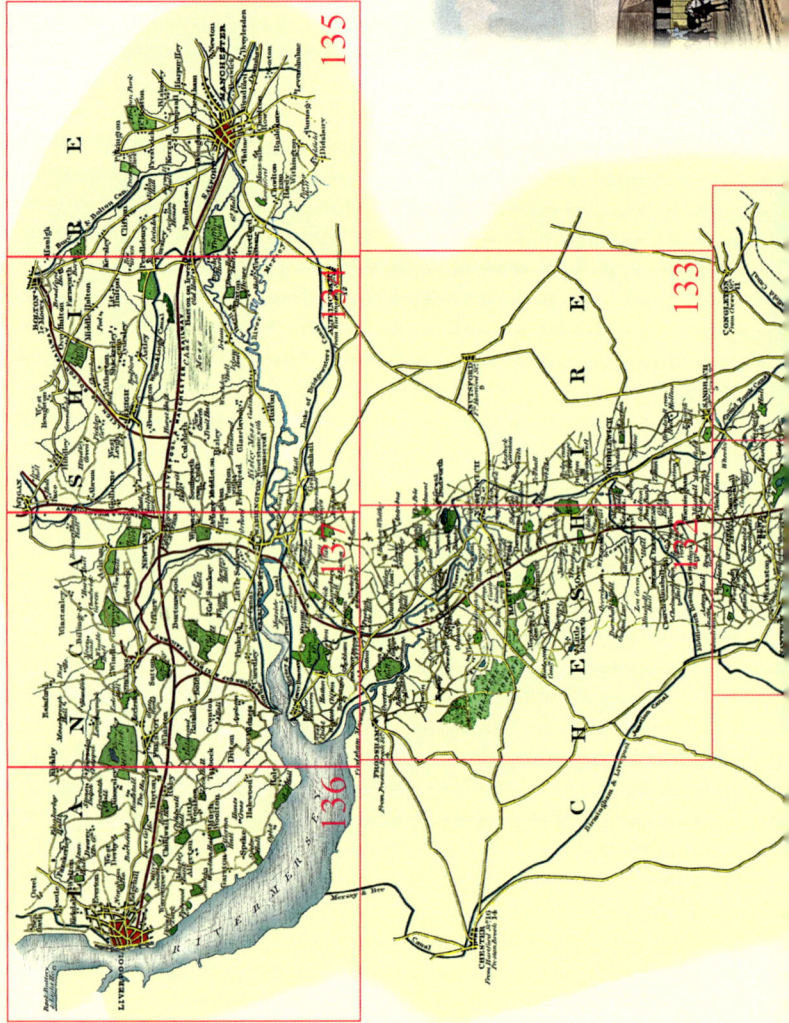

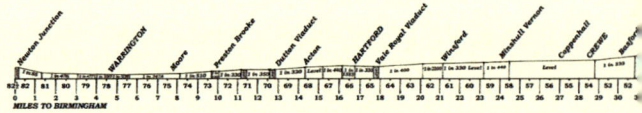

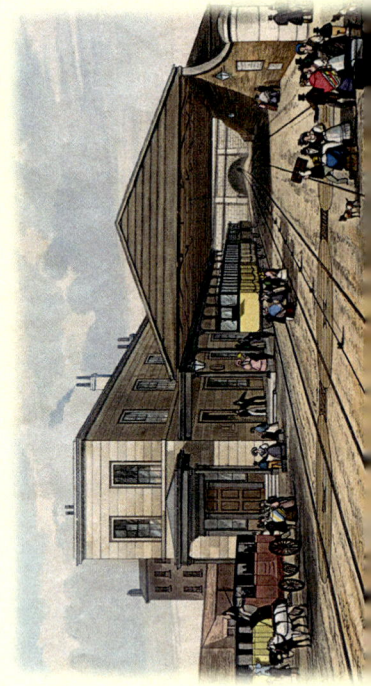

Tender

SECTION SHEWING THE INCLINATIONS OF THE LIVERPOOL & MANCHESTER RAILWAY.

LIVERPOOL   MANCHESTER

MILES TO BIRMINGHAM

135

134

133

137

134

136

Aston Church and Viaduct - Birmingham

Vauxhall - Birmingham Terminus of the Grand Junction Railway

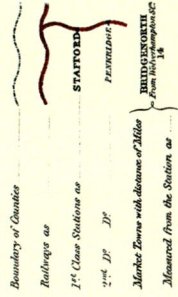

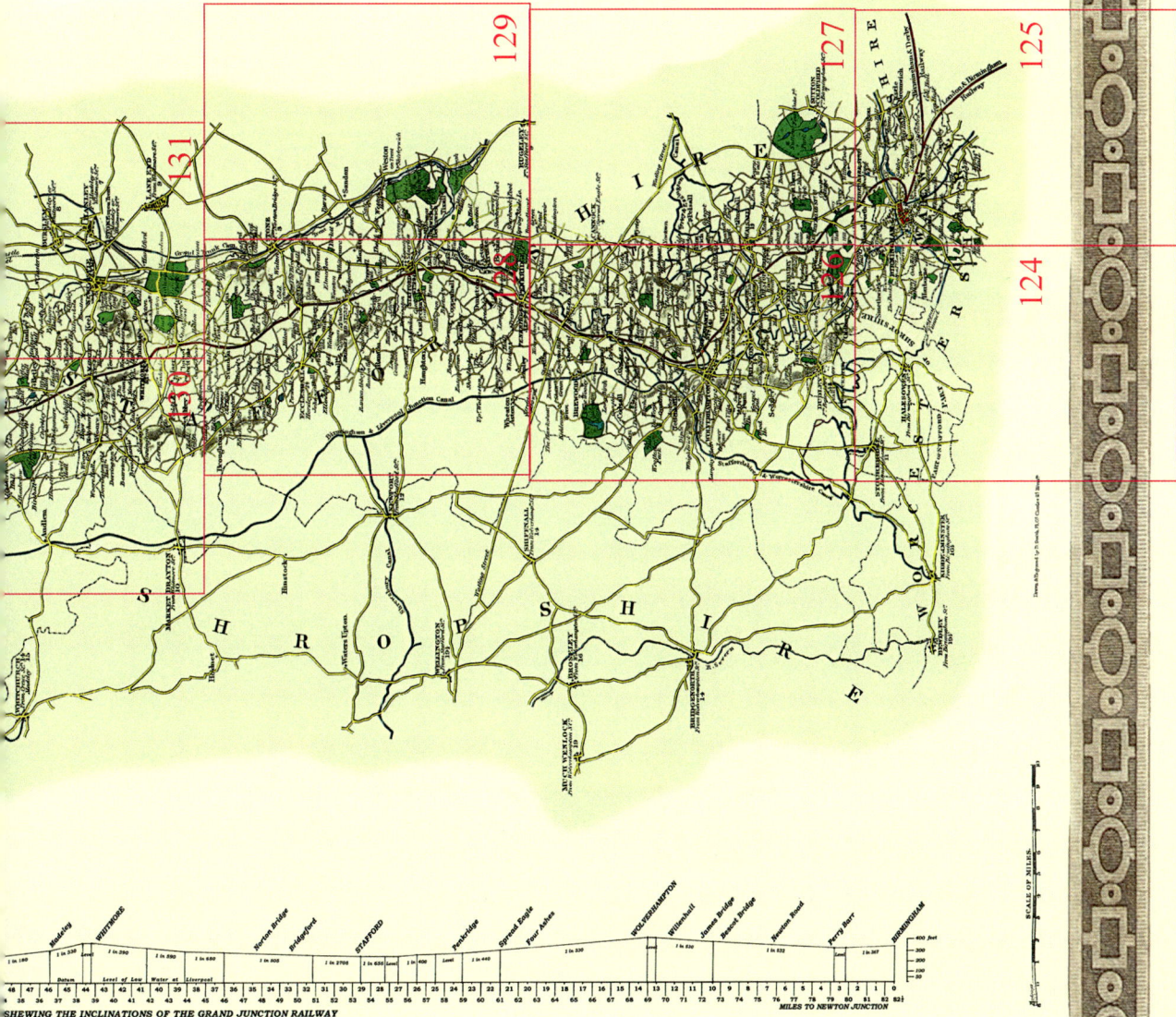

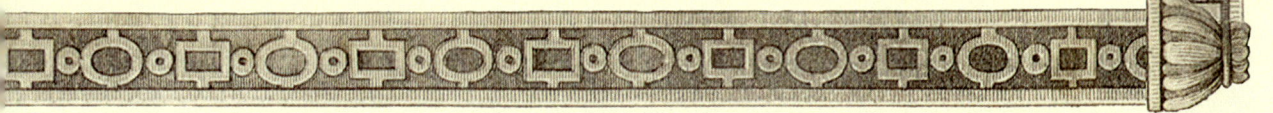

H.Harris. Del.

Boundary of Counties

Railways as

1st Class Stations as

2nd Do Do

Market Towns with distance of Miles

Measured from the Station as

STAFFORD

PENKRIDGE

BRIDGFORTH
from Wolverhampton &c.
14

131

129

130

128

127

126

124

125

S T A F F O R D S H I R E

S H R O P S H I R E

W O R C E S T E R S H I R E

SCALE OF MILES.

SHEWING THE INCLINATIONS OF THE GRAND JUNCTION RAILWAY

Badnley
WHITMORE
Norton Bridge
Bridgeford
STAFFORD
Penkridge
Spread Eagle
Four Ashes
WOLVERHAMPTON
Willenhall
James Bridge
Bescott Bridge
Newton Road
Perry Barr
BIRMINGHAM

MILES TO NEWTON JUNCTION

Datum   Level of Low Water at Liverpool

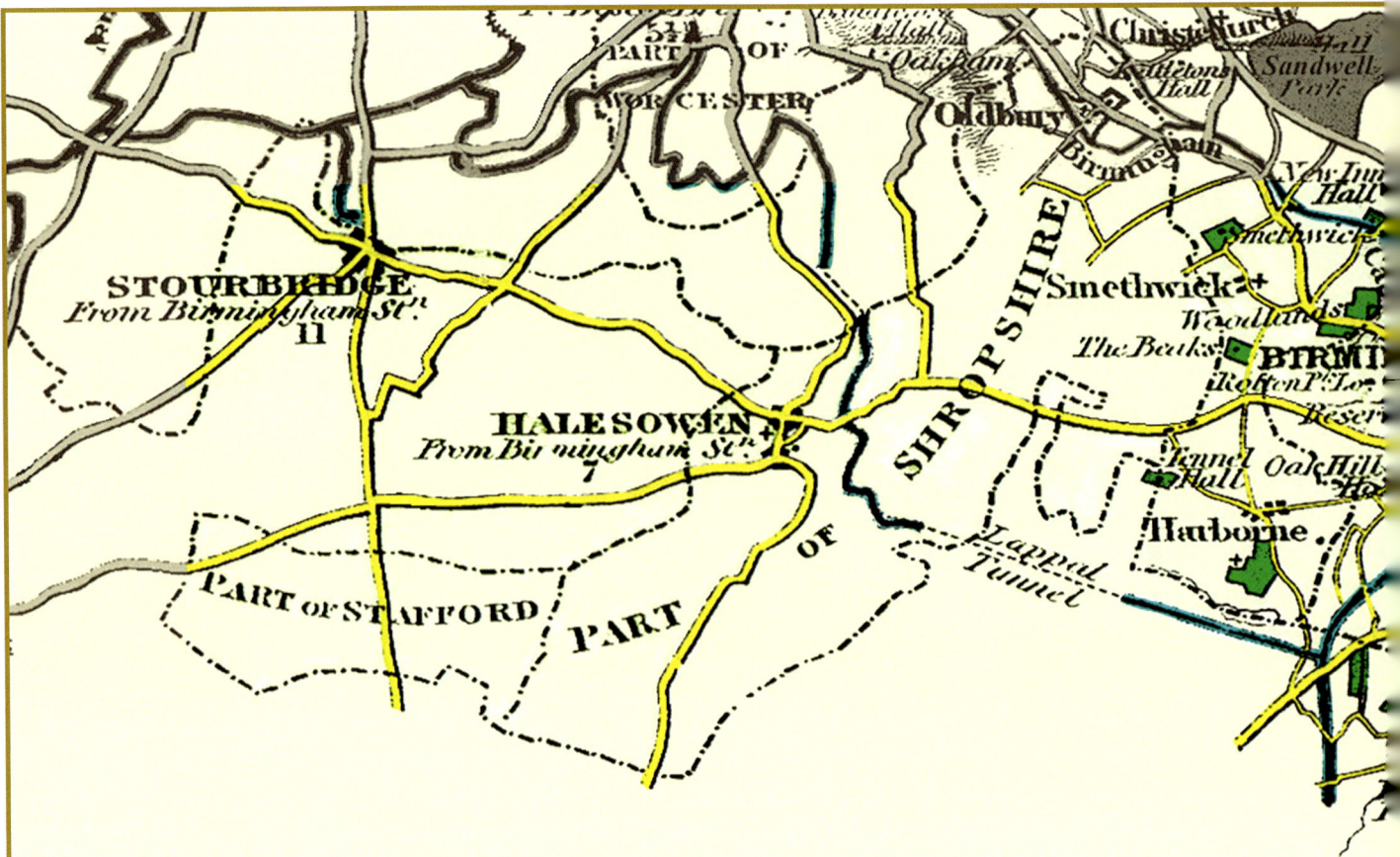

STOURBRIDGE
From Birmingham St. 11

HALESOWEN
From Birmingham St. 7

PART OF STAFFORD

PART OF SHROPSHIRE

PART OF WORCESTER

Oldbury

Christchurch

Sandwell Park

Smethwick

Woodlands

The Beaks

BIRMI

Oak Hill

Tunnel Hall

Harborne

Lappal Tunnel

SANDWELL HALL

124

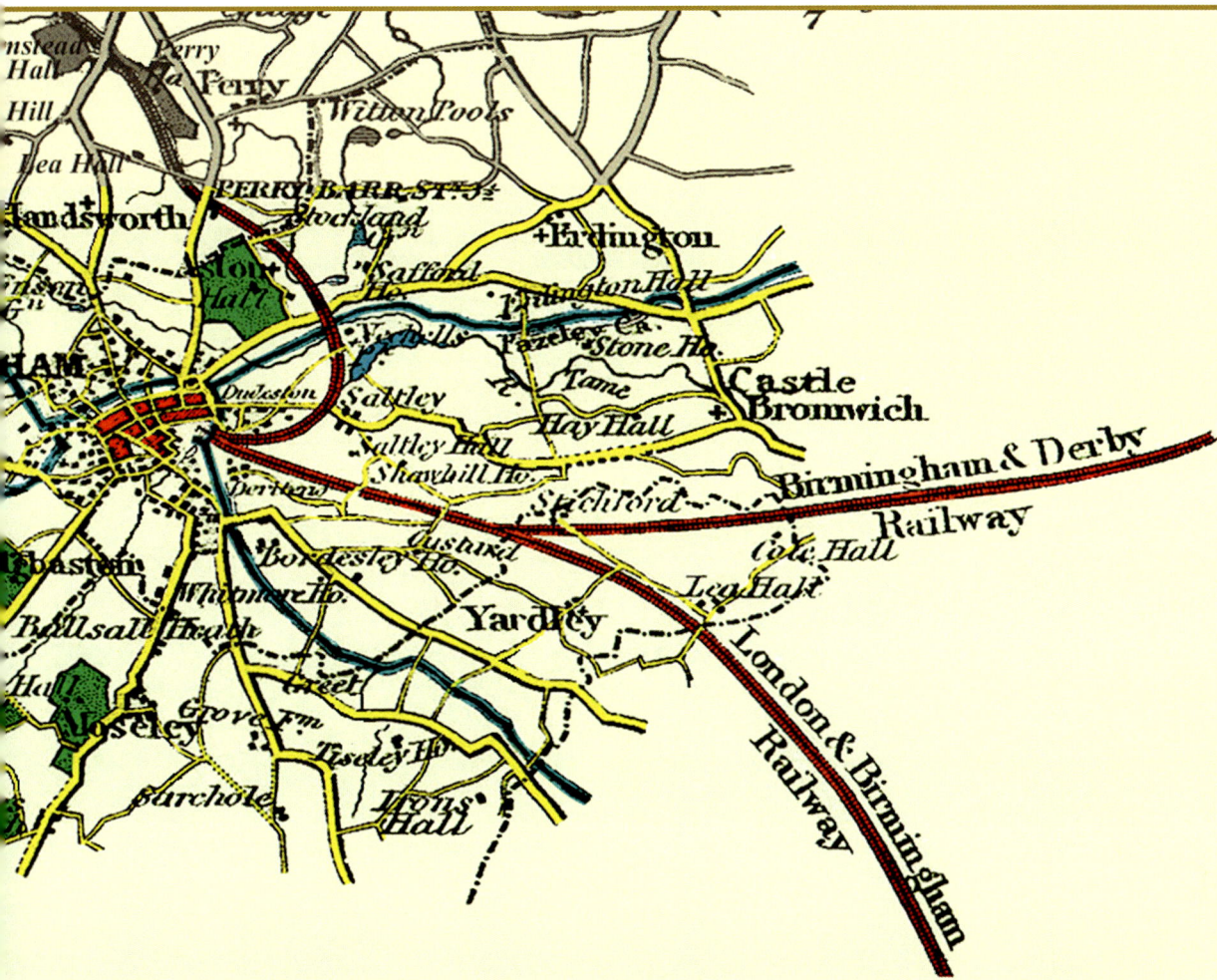

EDGBASTON HALL

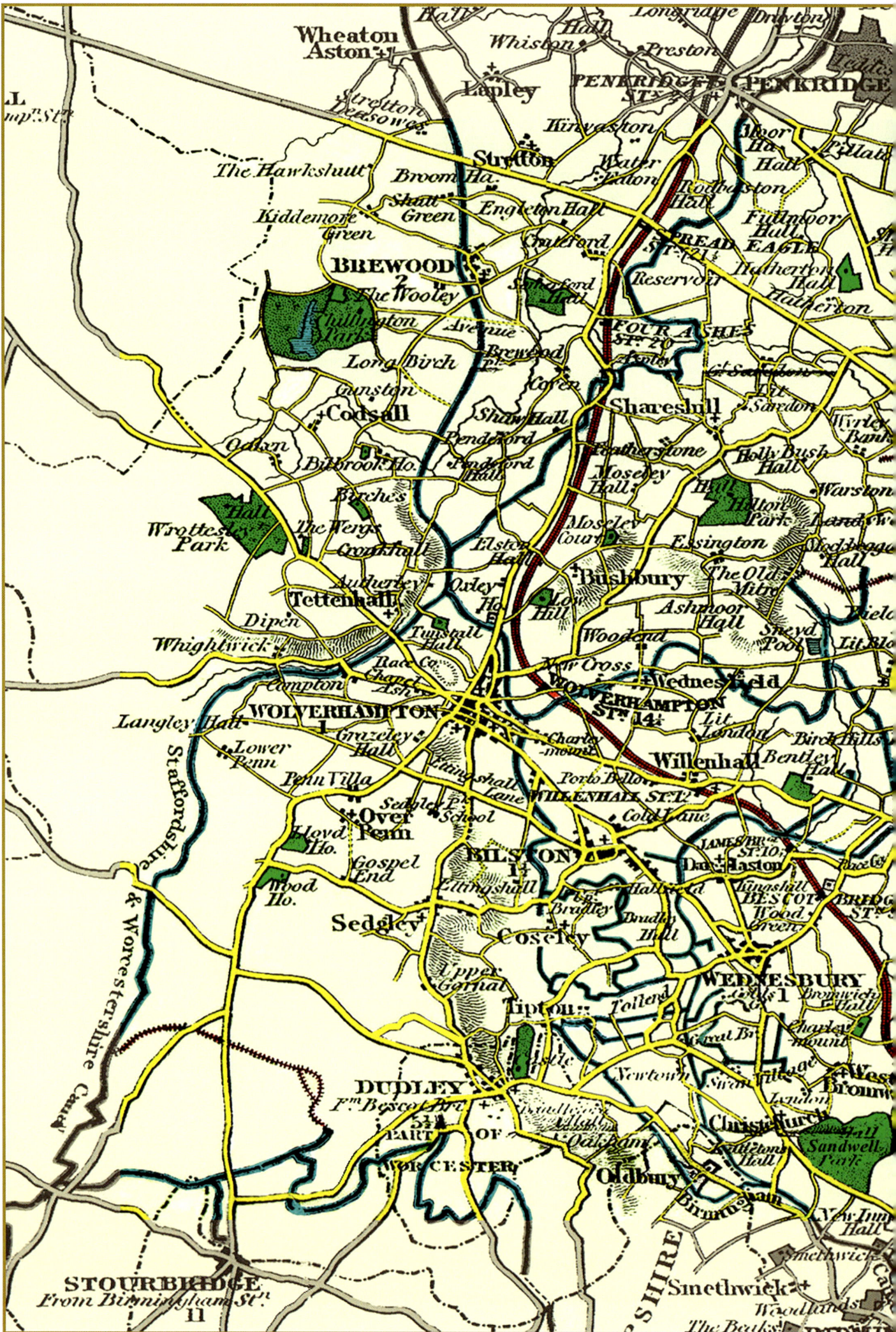

WHEATON ASTON

Whiston

Longridge

Preston

Lapley

PENKRIDGE STA 22

PENKRIDGE

Stretton Leasowes

Stretton

Water Eaton

Moor Hall

Hinkston

The Hawkshutt

Broom Ha.

Shutt Green

Engleton Hall

Rodbaston

Fullmoor Hall

Kiddemore Green

Cratford

SPREAD EAGLE STA 21

Hatherton Hall

BREWOOD

The Wooley

Soberford Hall

Reservoir

Hatherton

Chillington Park

Avenue

Long Birch

Brewood

FOUR ASHES STA 20

Coven

Gt. Saredon

Gunston

Shaw Hall

Shareshill

Sardon

Codsall

Pendeford

Featherstone

Holly Bush Hall

Wyrley Bank

Oaken

Pendeford Hall

Moseley Hall

Hilton Park

Warston

Bilbrook Ho.

Birches

Elston Hall

Moseley Court

Essington

The Old Mitre

Wrottesley Park

The Wergs

Oxley

Bushbury

Ashmoor Hall

Sheyd Pool

Crookhall

Oxley Ho.

Low Hill

Woodend

Lit. Blo

Tettenhall

Autherley

Dipen

Tunstall Hall

New Cross

Whightwick

Race Co.

Chapel Ash

WOLVERHAMPTON STA 14

WEDNESFIELD

WOLVERHAMPTON

Compton

Charles mount

Lit. London

Birch Hills

Langley Hall

Grazeley Hall

Ettingshall

WILLENHALL

Bentley Hall

Lower Penn

Penn Villa

Ettingshall Lane

Porto Bello

WILLENHALL STA 13

Cold Lane

Seabrd. L. School

JAMES BR. STA 10

Over Penn

Gospel End

BILSTON

Moxley Darlaston

BESCOT

BRIDGE

Hoyd Ho.

Wood Ho.

Ettingshall

Pitt. Bradley

Hall

Bradley Hall

Kingshall Wood Green

Sedgley

Coseley

Toilend

WEDNESBURY

Bromwich Hall

Upper Gornal

Tipton

Castle

Newtown

Charles mount

Swan Village

Lyndon

WEST BROMWICH

Fm. Bescot Bri.

DUDLEY

Bradley

Oakham

Christchurch

Sandwell Park

PART OF

WORCESTER

Oldbury

Knettleton Hall

Birmingham

New Inn Hall

SHIRE

Smethwick

STOURBRIDGE
From Birmingham St.
11

Woodlands

The Beaks

126

Sherbrook Pool
Spring Slade Lo.
Broadhurst Green
Pottal Reservoir
Huntington

RUGELEY
Frm Stafford Str
9

CANNOCK
Frm Spread Eagle Str
4

Wyrley

Watling Street

Canal

ewtown

Wyrley & Essington

Pelsall

Goscot Hall

Daw End

Rushall

WALSALL
14

Hill End

Bourne Vale

Red Ho.

Daffodilly

Hardwick

The Skip

Beacon

Great Barr

Barr Hall Park

Sutton Park

Fota

Oaks Pk

SUTTON COLDFIELD
Frm Birmingham Str
7

Kings

Oscott Cottage

Perry

Perry

Witton Pools

Erdington

PERRY BARR

andsworth

Stockland

Safford

Erdington Hall

Stone Ho.

THE GRAND JUNCTION AT PENKRIDGE

FOUR OAKS HALL

127

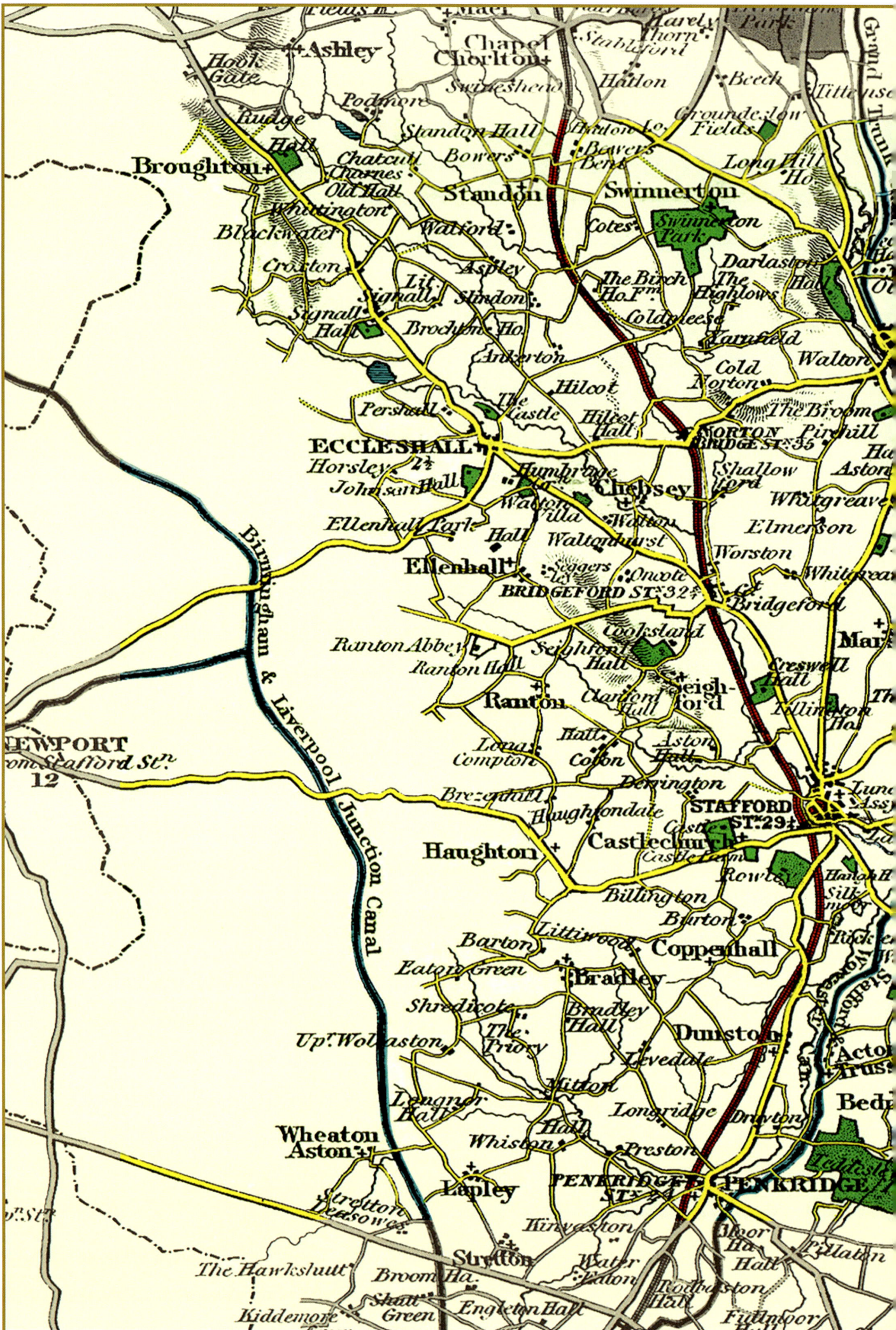

Hook
Gate
Ashley
+Maer
Chapel
Chorlton+
Stablford
Hanely
Thorn
PENKRIDE
Park
Grand Trunk
Tittens
Beech
Swineshead
Hatton
Groundslow
Long Hill
Rudge
Hall
Podmore
Standon Hall
Bowers
Dutton Ly
Fields
Ho
Bavers
Broughton+
Chatcull
Charnes
Old Hall
Standon
Cotes
Swinnerton
Darlaston
Swinnerton
Park
Walton
Watford
The Birch
Ho.Frm
The
Highlows
Whitington
Aspley
Blackwater
Coldmeese
Camfield
Croxton
Slindon
Lit
Signall
Brockton Ho.
Cold
Norton
Signall
Hall
Ankerton
Hilcot
The Broom
Pirhill
Pershall
The Castle
Hilcot
Hall
NORTON
BRIDGE St.35
Ha
ECCLESHALL
Aston
Horsley 2½
Johnson Hall
Humbridge
Shallow
Ford
Whitgreave
Chebsey
Elmerson
Ellenhall Park
Walton
Villa
Walton
Worston
Whitgrea
Hall
Waltonhurst
Ellenhall+
Seggers
ley
Onvote
Gt.
Bridgeford
Creswell
Hall
Mar
Ranton Abbey
BRIDGEFORD St.32¼
Coolesland
Hall
Ranton Hall
Seighfor
Hall
eigh-
ford
Tillington
Hall
The
NEWPORT
Ranton
Clanton
Hall
Aston
Stafford St.
12
Hall
Colton
Hall
Lower
Compton
Derrington
STAFFORD
St.29½
Luns
Ass
Brezenhill
Haughtondale
Castlechurch+
Castle Farm
Haughton+
Hanch H
Silk
Billington
Barton
Rowley
Act
Trust
Littiwood
Copenhall
Barton
Bed
Eaton Green
Bradley
Drayton
Shredicote
Bradley
Hall
Dunston
The
Priory
Levedale
Act
Trust
Up.Wollaston
Hitton
Longridge
Lengner
Hall
Hall
Preston
Drayton
Wheaton
Aston+
Whiston
Lapley
PENKRIDGE
St.14½
PENKRIDGE
Stretton
Densowes
Hinxaston
Shoor
Ha
Pillaton
The Hawkshutt
Broom Ha.
Stratton
Water
Eaton
Rodbaston
Hall
Kiddemore
Shutt
Green
Engleton Hall
Fidimoo

128

SWINNERTON HALL

STAFFORD

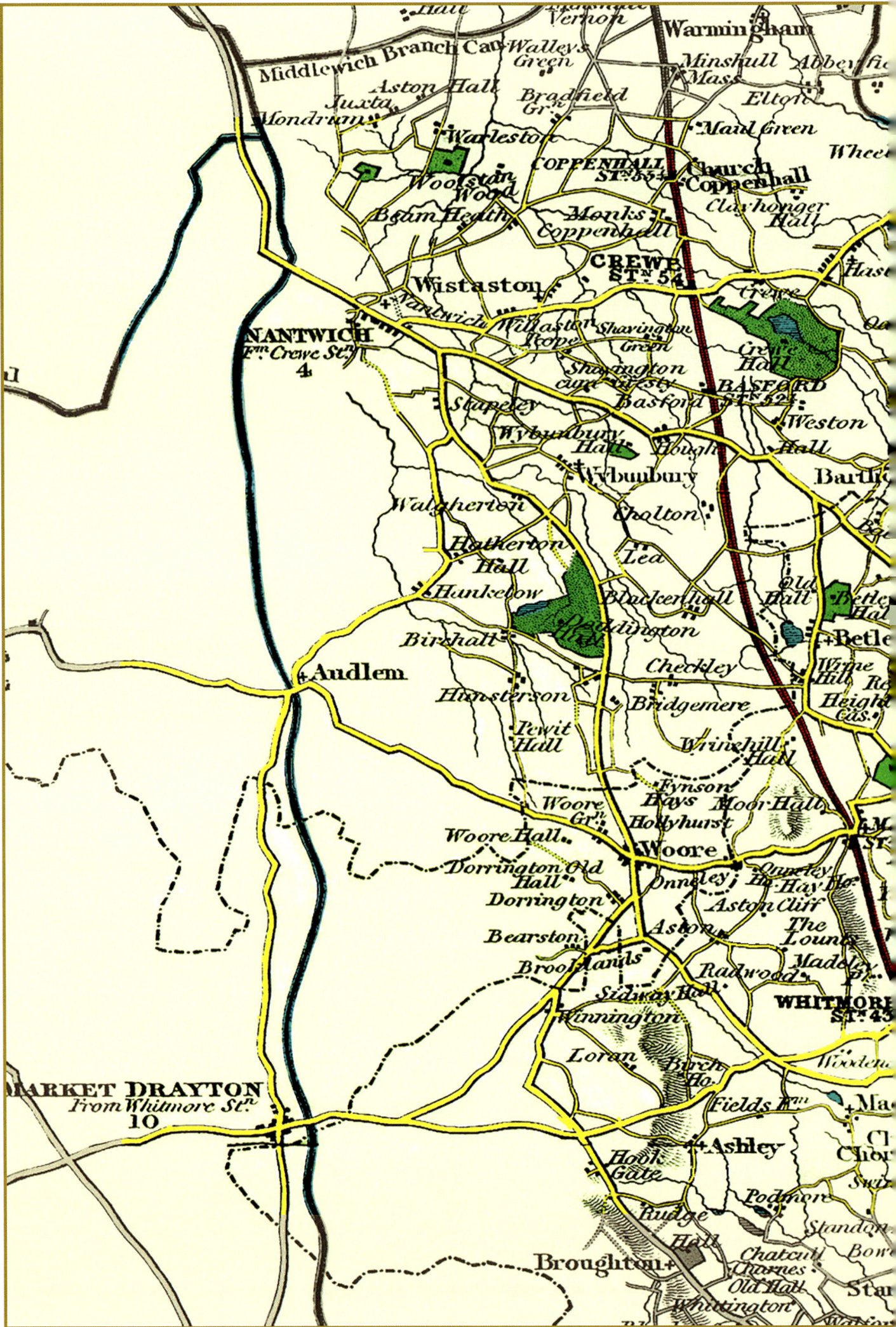

Middlewich Branch Ca.

Warmingham

Walleys Green

Aston Hall Juxta

Bradfield Gr.

Minshull Mass

Abber.field

Mondrum

Warleston

Maul Green

Elton

Wootston Wood

Beam Heath

COPPENHALL ST. 55½

Monks Coppenhall

Church Coppenhall

Clarhonger Hall

Wheel

CREWE ST. 54

Crewe

Wistaston

Crewe Hall

Hast

NANTWICH Fm. Crewe St. 4

Nantwich

Willaston Rope

Shavington green

BASFORD ST. 52½

Weston Hall

Stapeley

Shavington cum west.

Basford

Barthe

Wybunbury Hall

Hough

B

Watherton

Wybunbury

Weston

Cholton

Old Hall

Betle Hall

Hatherton Hall

Lea

Blackenhall

Betle

Hunkelow

Doddington Hall

Wime Hill Re.

Birshall

Checkley

Height Cas.

Audlem

Hunsterson

Bridgemere

Wrinehill Hall

Pewit Hall

Fynson Hays

Moor Hall

Woore Gr.

Hollyhurst

Woore Hall

Woore

Onneley

Dorrington Old Hall

Onneley Hy. Hay Ho.

Dorrington

Aston Cliff

The Lound

Bearston

Aston

Madely Br.

Broomhills

Radwood

WHITMORE ST. 43

Sidway Hall

Winnington

Loran

Birch Ho.

Wooden

MARKET DRAYTON From Whitmore St. 10

Fields Fm.

Ma

Ashley

Ch.

Hook Gate

Podmor

Chor

Rudge Hall

Standon

Bow

Broughton

Chatcull

Chrnes

Old Hall

Sta

Whittington

Water

130

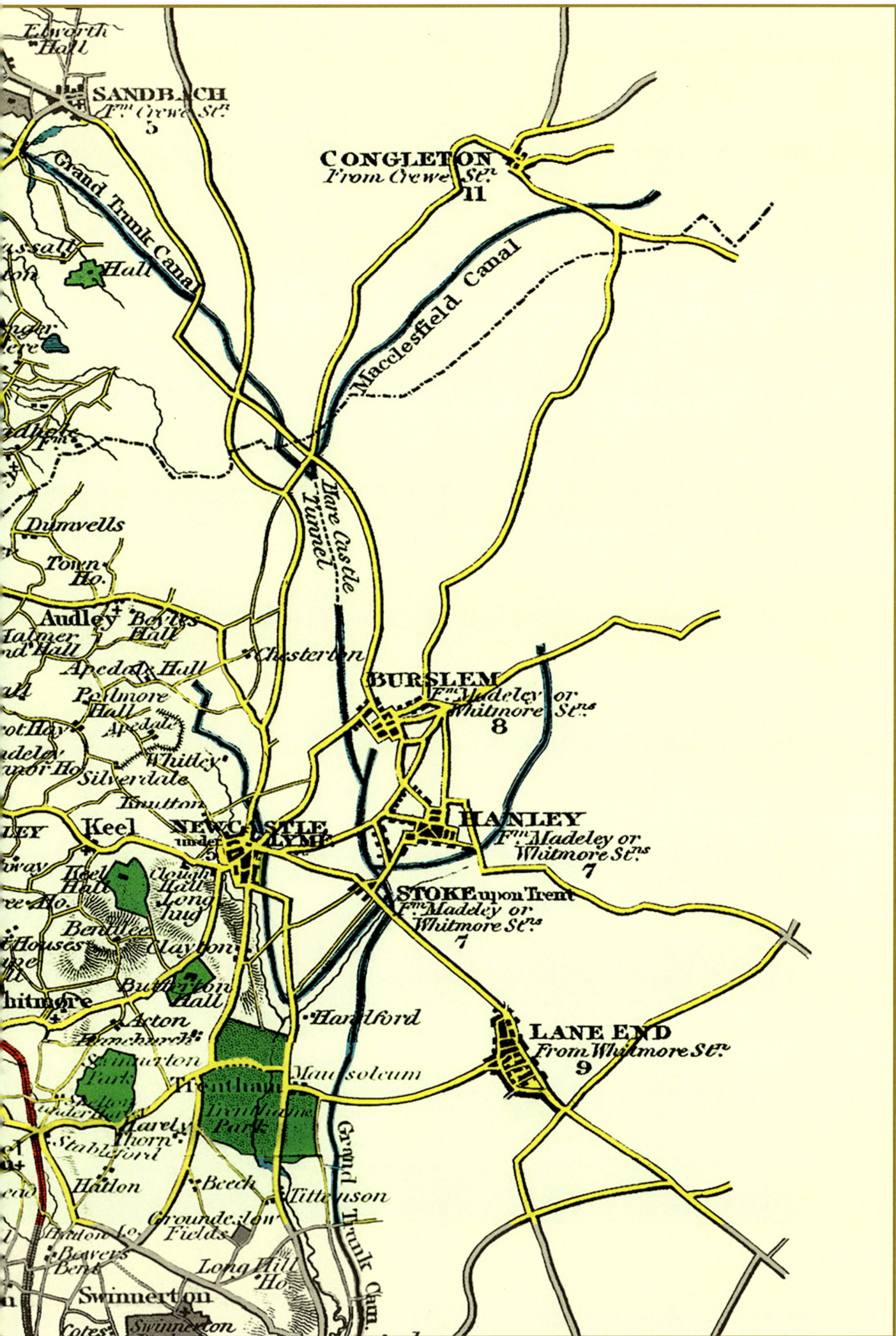

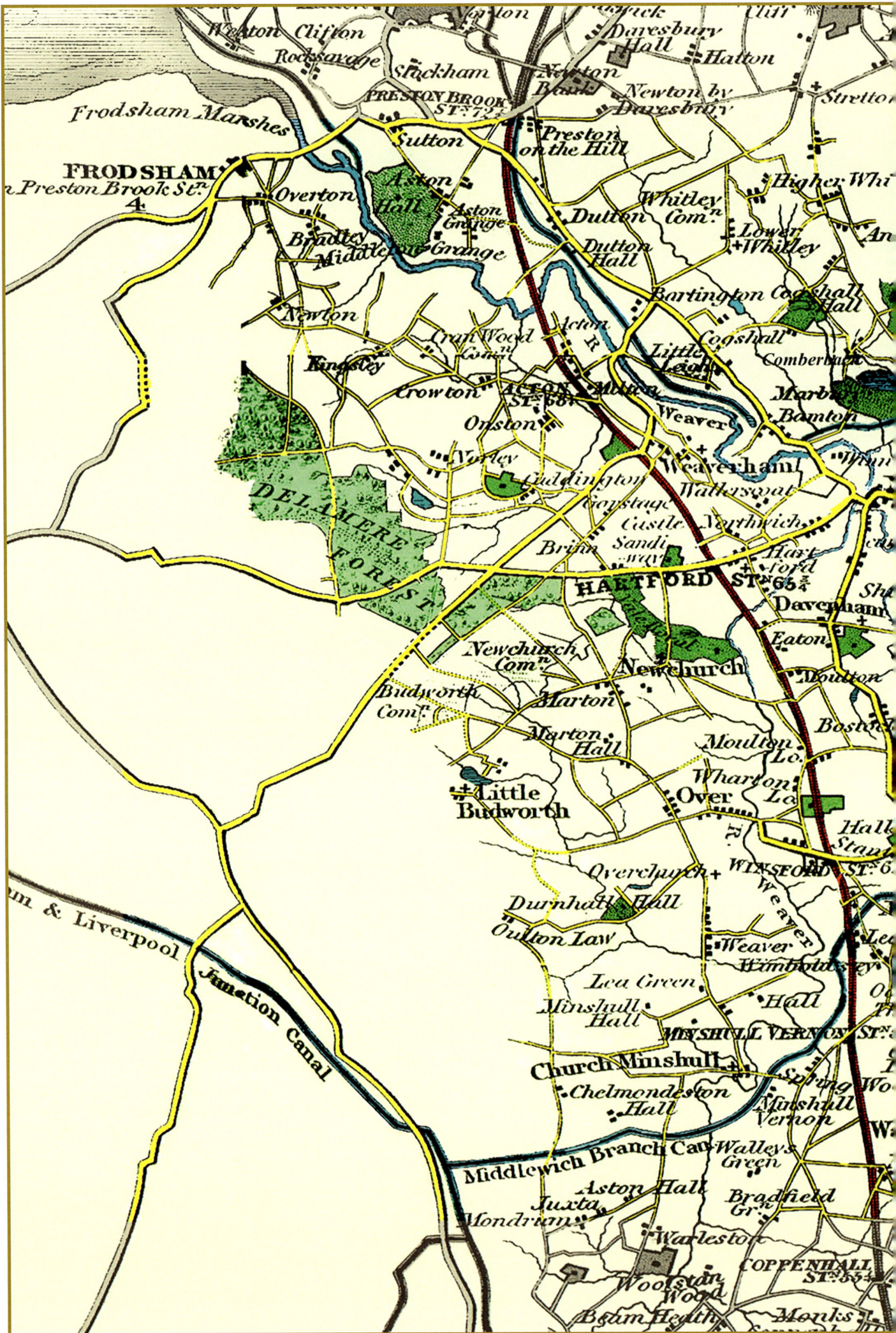

Weston Clifton
Rocksavage
Stockham
Newton
Daresbury
Hall
Hatton

PRESTON BROOK
ST. 72½
Newton
Bank
Newton by
Daresbury
Stretton

Frodsham Marshes
Sutton
Preston
on the Hill
Higher Whi

FRODSHAM
Overton
Aston
Hall
Aston
Grange
Dutton
Whitley
Com.
Lower
Whitley

n Preston Brook St.
4
Dutton
Hall
An

Bradley
Middleton Grange
Bartington Cogshall
Hall

Newton
Acton
Cogshall
Comberbach

Kingsley
Crar Wood
Com.
Little
Leigh
Marb

Crowton
ACTON
ST. 66½
Milton
Weaver
Bartion

Onston
Weaverham

Worley
Cuddington
Wallerscot
Winn

DELAMERE
Goystage
Castle
Northwich

FOREST
Brim
Sandiway
Hart-
ford
HARTFORD ST. 65¾

Davenham

Newchurch
Com.
Newchurch
Eaton

Budworth
Com.
Marton
Moulton

Marton
Hall
Bostl

Little
Budworth
Moulton
Lo.

Wharton
Lo.
Over

Overchurch
WINSFORD ST. 6
Hall
Stan

n & Liverpool
Durnhall Hall
Oulton Law
Weaver

Junction Canal
Lea Green
Wimboldsley

Minshull
Hall
Hall

MINSHULL VERNON ST.

Church Minshull
Spring Wo

Chelmondeston
Hall
Minshull
Vernon

Middlewich Branch Ca
Walleys
Green

Aston Hall
Juxta
Mondrum
Bradfield
Gr.

Warleston

Woolston
Wood
COPPENHALL
ST. 55¾

Bram Heath
Monks

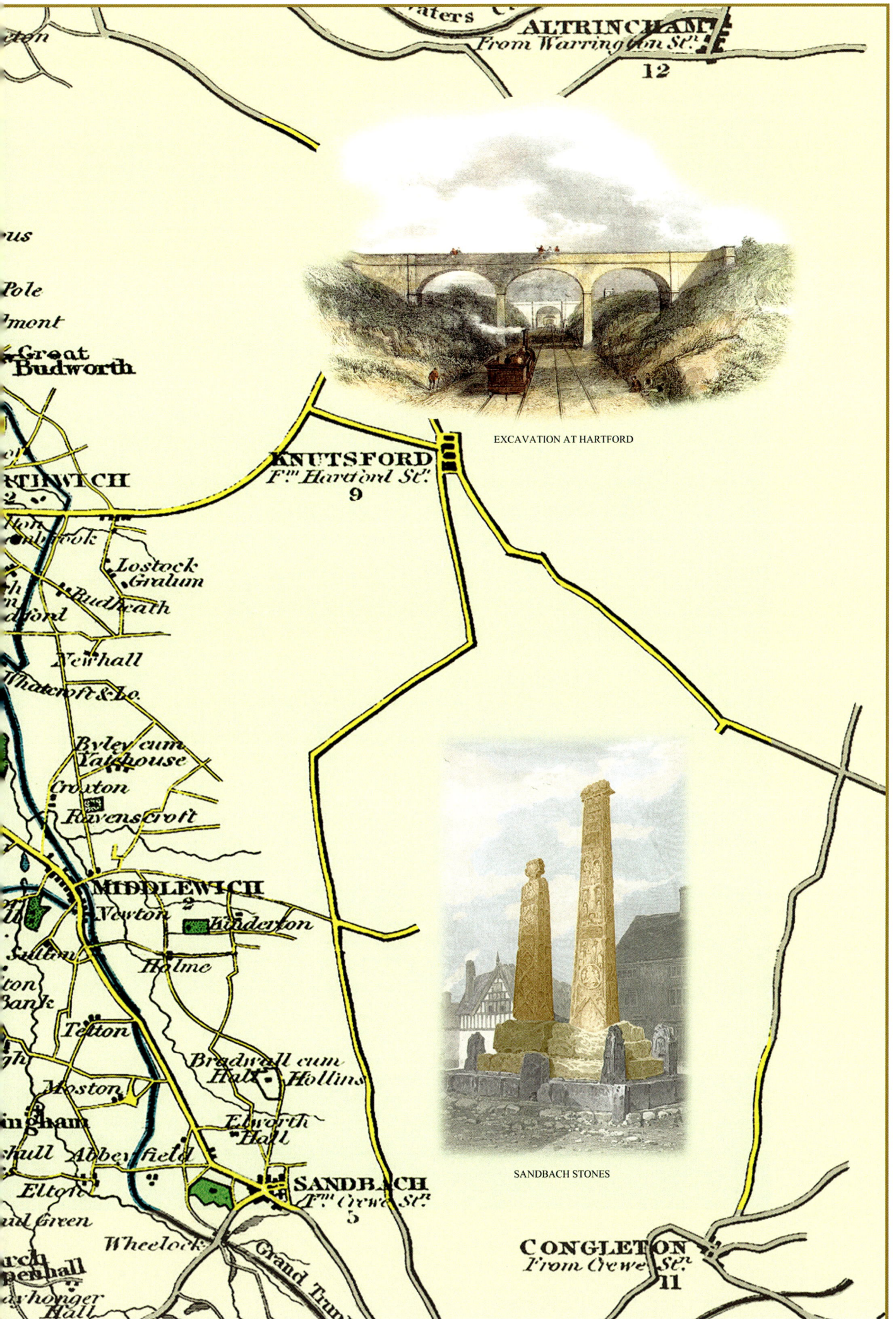

ALTRINCHAM
From Warrington St.
12

EXCAVATION AT HARTFORD

us
Pole
mont
Great
Budworth

KNUTSFORD
Fm Hartford St.
9

TTWICH

Lostock
Gralam
Budheath
Newhall
Thatcroft & Co.

Byley cum
Yatehouse
Croxton
Ravenscroft

MIDDLEWICH
Newton
Kinderton
Holme

Sutton
ton
Bank

Tetton
Bradwall cum
Hall
Hollins

Moston
Elworth
Hall

ingham
Abbeyfield

Elton
Green

Wheelock
Grand Trunk

SANDBACH
Fm Crewe St.
5

SANDBACH STONES

CONGLETON
From Crewe St.
11

133

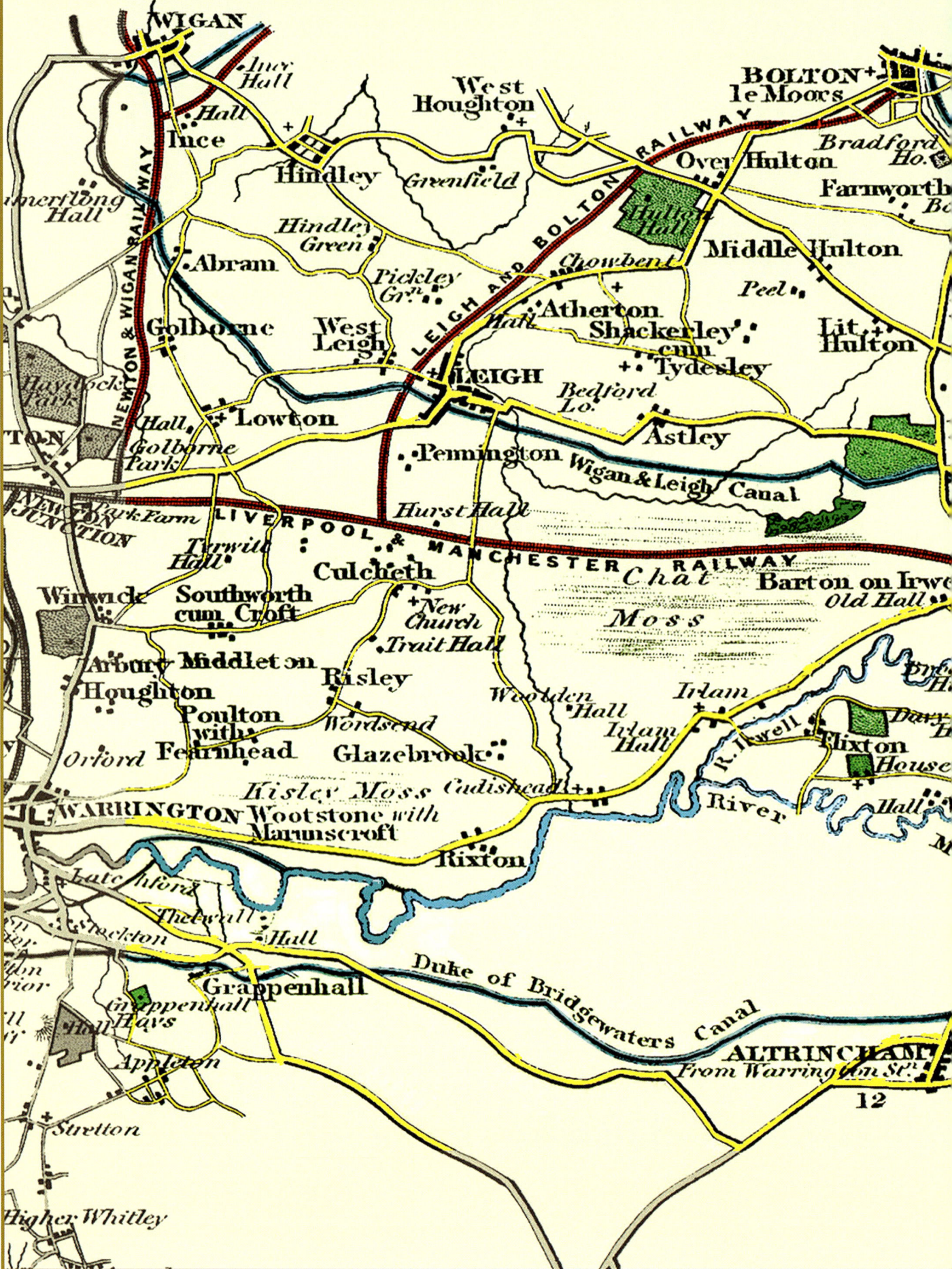

VIEW OF VICTORIA BRIDGE MANCHESTER

Haulgh

Bury

& Bolton Can.

sley

Clifton

en

dlebury

Swinton

orsley

Swinton
House

Clifton
Hall

Pendleton

Trafford
Park

me

G.t Hall

Stretford
stone

Longford

Moss-side

Chorlton
cum
Hardy

Barlow
Hall

Pilkington

Prestwich
Park

Heaton Park

Prestwich

G.t Heaton

Kersall
Hall

Kersall

Blakeley

Crumpsall

Harpur Hey

Broughton

Cheetham

SALFORD

Newton

MANCHESTER

Beswick

Droylesden

Hulme

Bradford

Openshaw

Chorlton
Row

Gorton

Rusholme

Withington

Levershulme

ey

Burnage

Parkfield

Didsbury

VIEW FROM THE CRESENT SALFORD

135

Rock Battery
& Light Ho.

Sea forth

Orrel

Fazakerley
Hall

Bootle

Fazakerley

Kirkdale

Walton

Walton
Hall

Dwerry
Ho. Gr.

Stone
Delph

Everton

Croxteth
Hall

Knowsle

LIVERPOOL

West
Derby

Newsham
Ho.

Barnfield

Rudstall
The Ha

Edgehill

Dove Cot
Ho.

Huyton

Olive
Mount

Wavertree

Childwall Ha

Rob

Dingle
Park

Mossley
Bank

Childwall
Hall

Little
Woolton

Futwood
Lo

Allerton

Sudeles
Woolton Hall

Much
Woolton

Garston

Allerton
Hall

Hunts
Cross

Speke

Halewood

Speke
Hall

Oglet

Ha

RIVER MERSEY

SHIPS OF WAR

Mersey & Dee

From Presta

136

WIGAN

Rainford

Mossborough Hall · Dial Ho.

Winstanley

by

Billinge

Bamerflong Hall

Ince

Hall

Blandfoot

Moss Bank

Hurst Hall

Chadwick Green

Abra

wsley

Longborough

Windle Hall

Ashton

Golbor

ppel

Eccleston Hall

Windle

Garswood Park

New Hall

Haydock Park

Hall

Knowsley Park

St HELENS

Haydock

Golborne Park

all Park

Eccleston

Glass Works

Sutton

Part

NEWTON

Newton Park Farm

PRESCOT

Whiston

Shirley Hall

Burtonwood

NEWTON JUNCTION

LI

Terw

Hall

Halsnead

Rainhill

Bold

Bold Hall

For Hall

Winwick

South cum C

St HELENS RAILWAY

Old Hall

Gr.t Sankey

Arbury

Middl

Cronton Hall

Whittle Hall

Bewsey Hall

Houghton

Poult with

Ditton

Appleton

Penketh

Little Sankey

Orford

Fearnh

Grove

Widness

RUNCORN GAP

Cuerdley

Sankey Canal

WARRINGTON ST.S

WARRINGTON

from Gap

Mossside Farm

Canal

Latchford

Thelwal

Mersey & Irwell

Acton Grange

Walton Inferior

Stockton

Lower Runcorn

MOORE ST.S

Walton Superior

Grap

Higher Runcorn

Norton Priory

The Elms

Hill Cliff

Appenhall Hays

Appleton

West Point

Hatton

Norton

Penkwick

Daresbury Hall

Hatton

Weston

Clifton

Rocksavage

Stockham

Newton Bank

Newton by Daresbury

Stretton

DSHAM Brook St.s 4.

PRESTON BROOK ST. 72½

Preston on the Hill

Sutton

Sham Marshes

Overton

Aston Hall

Aston Grange

Dutton

Whitley Com.n

Higher Whitley

(map labels as above)

PLACES TO VISIT TODAY

Apedale Valley Light Railway

Apedale Heritage Centre, Loomer Road, Chesterton, Staffordshire, ST5 7LB, Tel: 0845 0941953, Website: www.avlr.org.uk

There is something for everyone at Apedale. Young and old will enjoy a great value trip on a narrow gauge steam or diesel train alongside the Apedale Community Country Park.

Amerton Farm and Craft Centre

Amerton, Stowe by Chartley, Stafford, Staffordshire, ST18 0LA, Tel: 01889 270294, Website: www.amertonfarm.co.uk

Plenty to see in lovely surroundings. Tea Room, Craft Centre, Bakery and Farm Shop. Wonderful gifts and working crafts. Indoor adventure play area, farm yard, wildlife centre, summer steam train, garden centre and Children's parties.

Ancient High House

Greengate Street, Stafford, Staffordshire, ST16 2JA, Tel: 01785 619131, Website: www.staffordbc.gov.uk/heritage

Explore the museum set in England's largest remaining timber framed town house and visit the Civil War Room where Charles I stayed in 1642. Period room settings reflect the fascinating history of the house. School and group visits welcome. Extensive events programme, wedding venue and a Gift shop.

Aston Hall

Trinity Road, Aston, Birmingham, B6 6JD Tel: 0121 675 4722, Website: www.bmag.org.uk/aston-hall

Aston Hall is one of Birmingham's most treasured buildings. Aston Hall boasts sumptuous interiors from the 17th, 18th and 19th centuries, including the magnificent Long Gallery. Aston Hall and Park are hugely popular with family audiences and have a full programme of events, activities and trails throughout the season.

Biddulph Grange Garden   NT

Grange Road, Biddulph, Staffordshire, ST8 7SD, Tel: 01782 517999, Website: www.nationaltrust.org.uk/biddulph-grange-garden

Owned by the National Trust, one of Britain's most exciting and unusual gardens, with a series of connected compartments. Features a Chinese garden, Italian garden & Scottish Glen.

Black Country Museum

Black Country Living Museum, Tipton Road, Dudley, West Midlands, DY1 4SQ. Tel: 0121 557 9643, Website: www.bclm.co.uk

Our award-winning corner of the West Midlands is now one of the finest and largest open-air museums in the United Kingdom. With a village and charismatic residents to chat with. Trams to ride. Games to play. Things being made. Stories to hear. People – their triumphs to admire and troubles to be thankful that are not ours. Time to be well spent.

Borough Museum & Art Gallery

Brampton Park, Newcastle-under-Lyme, Staffordshire, ST5 0QP, Tel: 01782 619705, Website: www.newcastle-staffs.gov.uk

A victorian villa in parkland with local history galleries, varied temporary exhibits programme, family activities and events all year. Also craft shop, meeting room hire and schools service.

Chasewater Railway

Chasewater Country Park, Pool Road, Brownhills, Staffordshire, WS8 7NL, Tel: 01543 452623, Website: www.chasewaterrailway.org

Enjoy a 4 mile return railway journey in Chasewater Country park travelling in heritage steam and diesel trains. Great day out for the family with gift shops, cafes and fascinating railway museum.

Cheadle Discovery and Visitor Centre

Lulworth House, 51 High Street, Cheadle, Staffordshire, ST10 1AR, Tel: 01538 754157

The Discovery Centre is located in Lulworth House on the High Street, as well as a permanent display dedicated to AWN Pugin and the Hardman Company, there are exhibits and displays relating the heritage of the local area.

Churnet Valley Railway

Kingsley and Froghall Station, Froghall, Staffordshire, ST10 2HA, Tel: 01538 750755, Website: www.churnet-valley-railway.co.uk

The Churnet Valley Railway takes you on a journey back to the classic days of railway travel on a rural line that passes through beautiful countryside known as Staffordshire's "Little Switzerland".

Claymills Victorian Pumping Station

Meadow Lane, Stretton, Burton upon Trent, Staffordshire, DE13 0DA, Tel: 01283 509929, Website: www.claymills.org.uk

Fantastic steam beam engines. Stoke our steam boiler. Visit our steam driven workshop. Children can start a steam engine and blow the whistle.

Dudley Castle

Castle Hill, Dudley, West Midlands, DY1 4QF, Tel: 01384 215316 Website: www.dudleyzoo.org.uk/around-dzg/dudley-castle

The motte and bailey construction of Dudley Castle was completed in 1070 by Ansculf of Picardy. He was succeeded by the Paganel family during the 12th century who became Lords of Dudley. Today the castle and its courtyard are the scene of living demonstrations organised by re-enactment groups, along with our highly popular ghost walks which enter into the true spirit of the site — reputed to be haunted by the ghost of The Grey Lady – plus open-air music extravaganzas, children's events and amazing birds of prey displays.

Dudley Museum

Dudley Art Gallery and Museum, St James's Road, Dudley, DY1 1HU, Tel: 01384 815575, Website: www.dudley.gov.uk/see-and-do/museums/dudley-museum-art-gallery

Dudley Museum and Art Gallery provides a glimpse into Dudley's varied history and heritage. Local heroes like footballing legend Duncan Edwards can be seen side by side the museum's geological collection, which includes over 15,000 fossil, rock and mineral specimens. Combines permanent collections of art, geology and fossils with contemporary exhibitions, local interest shows and hands-on exhibitions related to the school curriculum.

Dudson Museum

Hope Street, Hanley, Stoke-on-Trent, Staffordshire, ST1 5DD, Tel: 01782 285286, Website: www.dudson.com

Discover the 213 year history of the oldest surviving family business in the ceramic tableware industry. Explore the original Dudson factory courtyard and bottle oven housing a wonderful collection of Dudson pottery.

Emma Bridgewater Factory

Lichfield Street, Stoke-on-Trent, Staffordshire, ST1 3EJ, Tel: 01782 201328, Website: www.emmabridgewaterfactory.co.uk

Enjoy a day out at our delightful Victorian working factory. Relax in the kitchen cafe by the Aga, Take a factory tour, Decorate your own masterpiece in the studio, Visit our little garden, Shop for factory seconds and amazing gifts.

Erasmus Darwin House

Beacon Street, Lichfield, Staffordshire, WS13 7AD, Tel: 01543 306260, Website: www.erasmusdarwin.org

Elegant Georgian home of Erasmus Darwin, grandfather of Charles Darwin. Located in idyllic surroundings. Period furnishings, interactive features and herb garden.

Ford Green Hall

**Ford Green Road, Smallthorne,
Stoke-on-Trent, Staffordshire, ST6 1NG,
Tel: 01782 537696,
Website: www.stoke.gov.uk/museum**

Home to the Ford Family for nearly 200 years, Ford Green Hall is a 17th century timber-framed farmhouse, complete with period garden offering visitors a fascinating insight into the life of the 17th century.

Foxfield Steam Railway

**Caverswall Road, Blythe Bridge,
Stoke-On-Trent, Staffordshire, ST11 9BG,
Tel: 01782 396210,
Website: www.foxfieldrailway.co.uk**

An industrial heritage steam railway operating steam train journeys through beautiful North Staffordshire countryside. Museum housing extensive collection of steam locomotives. Tearoom, bar and shop available. Special events calendar.

Gladstone Pottery Museum

**Uttoxeter Road, Longton, Stoke-on-Trent,
Staffordshire, ST3 1PQ, Tel: 01782 237777,
Website: www.stoke.gov.uk/museum**

The only complete Victorian pottery factory with original workshops, huge bottle ovens, cobbled yard, tile gallery, Doctor's House and Flushed with Pride - the story of the toilet. Visit the gift shop for handmade pottery, books and gifts.

Izaak Walton's Cottage

**Worston Lane, Shallowford, Stafford,
Staffordshire, ST15 0PA, Tel: 01785 760278,
Website: www.staffordbc.gov.uk/heritage**

Thatched timberframed 16th century Cottage bequeathed to the people of Stafford by Izaak Walton, the celebrated author of "the Compleat Angler". The cottage is home to a small angling museum.

Lichfield Heritage Centre

**St. Mary's Centre, Breadmarket Street,
Lichfield, Staffordshire, WS13 6LG,
Tel: 01543 256611,
Website: www.lichfieldheritage.org.uk**

Set in the beautiful venue of St. Mary's Church, Lichfield Heritage Centre combines a fascinating exhibition with a coffee shop and gift shop.

Marston's Visitor Centre

**Marston's Brewery, Shobnall Road,
Burton upon Trent, Staffordshire, DE14 2BG,
Tel: 01283 507391,
Website: www.marstonsbeercompany.co.uk**

Tour the only working brewery in the world still brewing cask beer using the traditional Burton Union method, where the famous Marston's Pedigree is fermented in oak casks.

Moorcroft Heritage Visitor Centre

**Sandbach Road, Burslem, Stoke-on-Trent,
Staffordshire, ST6 2DQ, Tel: 01782 820515,
Website: www.moorcroft.com**

Described as the worlds best kept secret, a visit will reveal Moorcroft's unique handcrafted, quality, collectable art pottery. Factory tours, shopping, museum and bottle oven come together creating an unforgettable experience.

Moseley Old Hall   NT

**Moseley Old Hall Lane, Fordhouses,
Wolverhampton, West Midlands, WV10 7HY,
Tel: 01902 782808, Website: www.nationaltrust.
org.uk/moseley-old-hall**

Tread in the footsteps of a king at this atmospheric Elizabethan farmhouse, which holds many secrets. Charles II hid here whilst fleeing for his life after the Battle of Worcester in 1651. Visit the 17th century garden, tearoom, shop and events.

Museum of Cannock Chase

**Valley Road, Hednesford, Staffordshire,
WS12 1TD, Tel: 01543 877666,
Website: www.wlct.org/museumofcannockchase**

The Museum of Cannock Chase illustrates the rich social and industrial heritage of the Cannock Chase area.

National Memorial Arboretum

Croxall Road, Alrewas, Burton-on-Trent, Staffordshire, DE13 7AR, Tel: 01283 792333, Website: www.thenma.org.uk

150 acres of trees and memorials, planted as a living tribute to those who have served, died or suffered in the service of their Country. Including a Chapel, Visitor Centre, Cafe & Shop.

Nicholson Gallery and Museum

1st Floor, Nicholson Institute, Moorlands House, Stockwell Street, Leek, ST13 6DW, Tel: 01538 395456, Website: www. staffsmoorlands.gov.uk/nicholson

The Nicholson Gallery is housed within the Nicholson Institute and is a living example of late Victorian philanthropy. The Gallery features a mixed programme of community based exhibitions and local history.

The Old Guildhall Prison Cells

The Guildhall, Bore Street, Lichfield, Staffordshire, WS13 6LX, Tel: 01543 264972, Website: www.lichfield.gov.uk

Explore the city's Old Prison on this site since 1548. See original cells, discover the inmates stories and find out about law and order in Lichfield in this small display.

Royal Air Force Museum

Cosford, Shifnal, Shropshire, TF11 8UP, Tel: 01902 376200, Website: www.rafmuseum.org.uk/cosford

Royal Air Force Museum Cosford has a collection of 70 historic aircraft and the National Cold War Exhibition. Includes restaurant, shop hands on gallery, simulator and 4D experience.

St John's Hospital and Chapel

St. John Street, Lichfield, Staffordshire, WS13 6PB, Tel: 01543 264169, Website: www.stjohnslichfield.com

The Hospital, a place of hospitality and now providing sheltered housing for retired people is one of the finest 15th Century brick buildings in the Country. There is a magnificent stained glass window in the ancient chapel, built in 1135.

Samuel Johnson Birthplace Museum

Breadmarket Street, Lichfield, Staffordshire, WS13 6LG, Tel: 01543 264972, Website: www.samueljohnsonbirthplace.org.uk

Birthplace of Dr Johnson, the leading literary figure of his day. Follow the story of his life from childhood to his dictionary fame.

Shire Hall Gallery

Market Square, Stafford, Staffordshire, ST16 2LD, Tel: 01785 278345, Website: www.staffordshire.gov.uk/arts

The Shire Hall Gallery is housed in the heart of Stafford Town Centre. The Gallery consists of a large, temporary exhibition sapce, craft council select craft shop and historic court room.

The Shugborough Estate

Shugborough Estate, Milford, Stafford, ST17 0XB Tel: 0845 459 8900, Website: www.shugborough.org.uk

Step back in time at the historic working estate of Shugborough and enjoy a living experience brought to life by costumed characters straight from the pages of Shugborough's very own history books. Mansion House, Servants' Quarters, Working Farm & Mill, Riverside Gardens, Park & Land Train Ride, Restaurant & Craft Shops. Shugborough Revisited including the Earls private apartments open for the first time ever, interactive galleries, island arboretum and sculpture trail, Patrick Lichfield Photographic Exhibition

Soho House

Soho Avenue, Handsworth Birmingham, B18 5LB, Tel: 0121 5549122 , Website: www.bmag.org.uk/soho-house

Soho House was the elegant home of industrialist and enterpreneur Matthew Boulton from 1766 to 1809. Carefully restored, this fashionable Georgian house features period room interiors with fine collections of ormolu, silver, furniture and paintings. It was once a regular meeting place for some of the greatest minds of the 18th century. Matthew Boulton (1728–1809) was a founding member of the Lunar Society, a group of great thinkers and inventors who met regularly at his home at Soho

Spode Works Visitor Centre

Elenora Street, Stoke-on-Trent, Staffordshire, ST4 1QQ, Tel: 01782 792525, Website: www.spodeworks.org

Celebrate the heritage of one of the most famous factories of the Industrial Revolution; the birthplace of bone china. An exhibition showcasing amazing artefacts, film, activities and stories from the former Spode site.

Stafford Castle

Newport Road, Stafford, Staffordshire, ST16 1DJ, Tel: 01785 257698, Website: www.staffordbc.gov.uk/heritage

Discover 900 years of history. Originally a Motte and Bailey castle, the stone keep was destroyed during the Civil War.

Sugnall Walled Kitchen Garden

Sugnall, Stafford, Staffordshire, ST21 6NF, Tel: 01785 850820, Website: www.sugnall.co.uk

Explore the 2-acre historic walled kitchen garden that dates back to 1737. Over the last 6 years the current owners have brought the walled garden back into production and have opened a tea room and garden shop.

Tamworth Castle

Tamworth, Staffordshire, B79 7NA, Tel: 01827 709629, Website: www.tamworthcastle.co.uk

Tamworth Castle is the number one Heritage attraction located in the town. Explore over 900 years of history in the magnificent Motte and Bailey Castle. The Ancient Walls hold many secrets from sieges, haunting, royal visits and bankruptcy.

The National Brewery Centre

Horninglow Street, Burton upon Trent, Staffordshire, DE14 1NG, Tel: 01283 532880, Website: www.nationalbrewerycentre.co.uk

The National Brewery Centre celebrates Burton upon Trent's proud brewing heritage and its influence worldwide. Visitors are told the story of brewing by actors in period costume, multi-media interactive displays and hundreds of exhibits.

The Potteries Museum & Art Gallery

Bethesda Street, City Centre, Stoke-on-Trent, Staffordshire, ST1 3DW, Tel: 01782 232323, Website: www.stoke.gov.uk/museum

Discover the world famous Staffordshire Hoard along with the history of the Potteries, including the world's greatest collection of Staffordshire Ceramics. See a Spitfire and all sorts of art and craft.

Trentham Gardens

The Trentham Estate, Stone Road, Trentham, Stoke-on-Trent, Staffordshire ST4 8JG, Tel: 01782 646646, Website: www.trentham.co.uk

Trentham Gardens is located at The Trentham Estate, where you'll also find Trentham Monkey Forest, Aerial Extreme and a beautiful timber lodge Shopping Village with over 60 shops cafes and restaurants.

Walsall Leather Museum

Littleton Street West, Walsall, WS2 8EQ, Tel: 01922 721153, Website: www.walsall.gov.uk/leathermuseum

Discover why Walsall became the British leather goods capital in this fascinating working museum, housed in a restored leather factory. For two hundred years Walsall people have been making some of the world's finest saddles and leather goods. Walsall Leather Museum seeks to celebrate this great tradition and reflect the achievements of the leather craftsmen and women of Walsall.

Wedgwood Visitor Centre & Museum

Wedgwood Drive, Barlaston, Stoke-on-Trent, Staffordshire, ST12 9ER, Tel: 01782 282986, Website: www.wedgwoodvisitorcentre.com

At the Home of Wedgwood enjoy a guided tour around the working factory, explore our award winning interactive Museum and even have a go on the potter's wheel! Include shopping and dining and there's something for the whole family.

PICTURE CREDITS

Osborne's Map of The Grand Junction Railway and town plans featured throughout
© Mapseeker Archive Publishing Ltd
www.mapseeker.co.uk
www.oldmapsandimages.co.uk

With special thanks to

Wolverhampton Art Gallery Collections

The Church of St Giles Willenhall © WAVE Wolverhampton Art Gallery – Page 49

National Railway Museum

The Wildfire Steam Engine © Science & Society Picture Library – Page 144

The Black Country from the Fox Sketch Book – Courtesy Dudley Museum – Pages 8–9

Images of Curzon Street Station – © John Alsop Collection – Page 21

Pictorial images views, vistas and other artefacts.

Mapseeker Archive Publishing Ltd

With special thanks to the following in the sourcing of antique original resources art worked for this atlas publication

Berian Williams Antique Maps and prints
www.antique-prints-maps.co.uk

Steve Bartrick Maps and prints
www.antiqueprints.com

Arthur Hook Old Maps and Books
www.hooksbooks.co.uk

Mary Evans Picture Library
www.maryevans.com

All of the Early Town Plans featured in this atlas are available as photographic prints and in a range of other products on **www.mapseeker.co.uk** and **www.oldmapsandimages.co.uk**

DEDICATION TO THE WILDFIRE

The image illustrated above is of the model (our inventory number at the National Railway's Museum Collection 1975–7911) that was made by John Stagg of Birmingham in 1839. It represents Wildfire, the first northbound train to leave Birmingham on the Grand Junction Railway on 4th July 1837. It is of very fine workmanship and accurate in many details, but as it was built for live steaming the boiler, it has a large central flue rather than many small firetubes. The records of the original engine are sparse, but the model is actually too narrow and probably too long, as the scaled dimensions do not match those of similar locomotives built by Robert Stephenson & Co. The model is 39cm tall and is in approximately 1/10 scale.

The model shows that Wildfire was of the Patentee type, with outside sandwich frames and four inside frames running from the cylinders to crank axle. The cylinders are in the bottom of the smokebox, with valves on top. There is a water pump for boiler feed on each side of the engine, driven by the crosshead.

The provenance of the model is uncertain, but by the 1950s it was owned by British Railways London Midland Region and later became part of the Museum of British Transport and then National Railway Museum collections.

Ed Bartholomew
National Railway Museum

www.nrm.org.uk

RECOMMENDATIONS

Mapseeker Books – Armchair Time Travellers Street Atlas Series

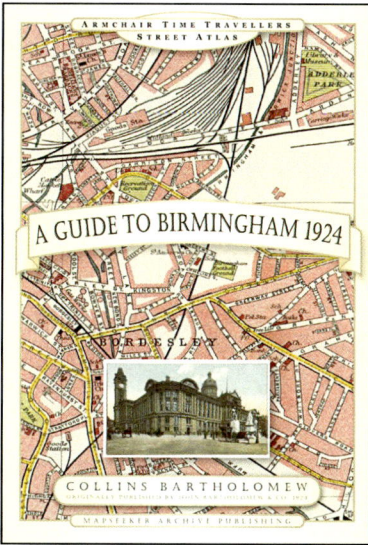

A GUIDE TO BIRMINGHAM 1924
Hardcover: ISBN 9781844918225 £19.99

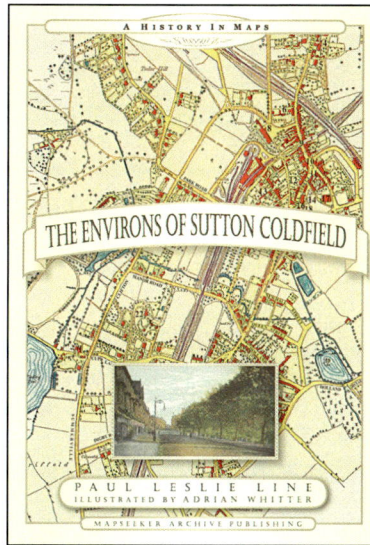

THE ENVIRONS OF SUTTON COLDFIELD
A HISTORY IN MAPS
Hardcover: ISBN 9781844917808 £19.99

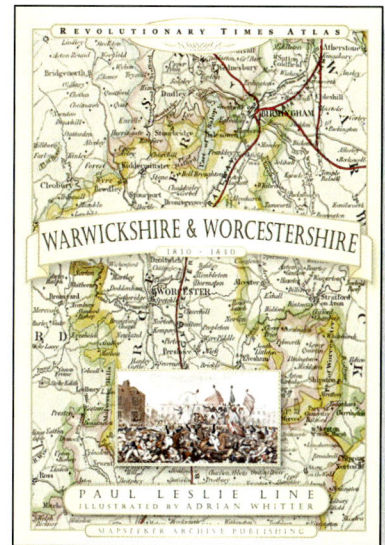

REVOLUTIONARY TIMES ATLAS OF
WARWICKSHIRE AND WORCESTERSHIRE
1830–1840
Hardcover: ISBN 9781844917457 £19.99

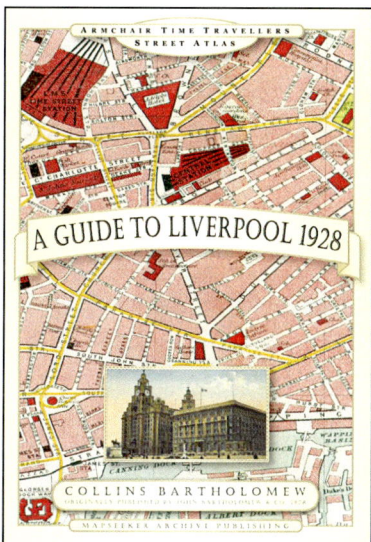

A GUIDE TO LIVERPOOL 1928
Hardcover: ISBN 9781844918218 £19.99

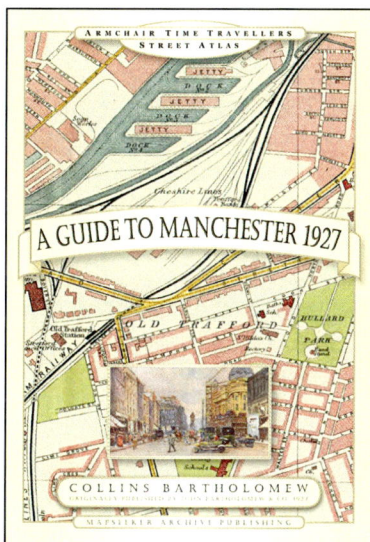

A GUIDE TO MANCHESTER 1927
Hardcover: ISBN 978-1844918201 £19.99

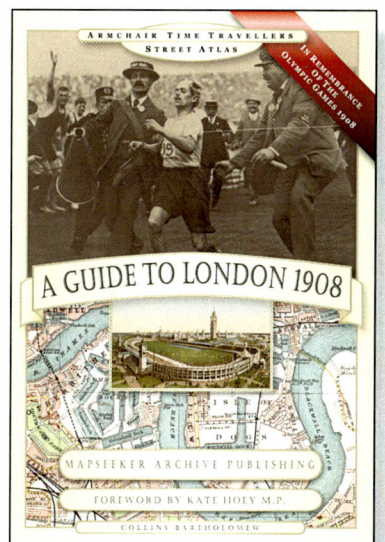

A GUIDE TO LONDON 1908
Hardcover: ISBN 9781844917891 £19.99

Mapseeker Birmingham Historic Maps Collection

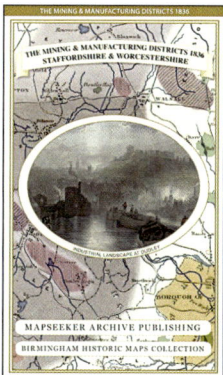

MINING & MANUFACTURING
DISTRICTS 1836 – STAFFORD-
SHIRE & WORCESTERSHIRE:
ISBN 9781844918188 £14.99

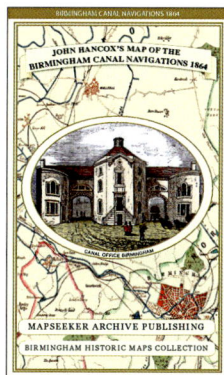

JOHN HANCOX'S MAP OF
THE BIRMINGHAM CANAL
NAVIGATIONS 1864:
ISBN 9781844918126 £14.99

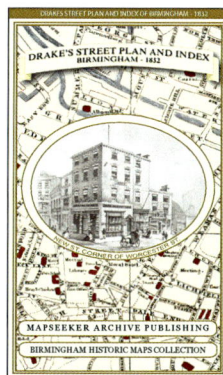

JAMES DRAKES STREET
PLAN AND INDEX OF
BIRMINGHAM 1832:
ISBN 9781844918133 £14.99

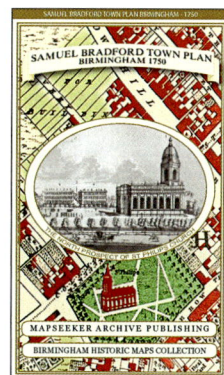

SAMUEL BRADFORD TOWN
PLAN BIRMINGHAM 1750:
ISBN 9781844918089 £14.99

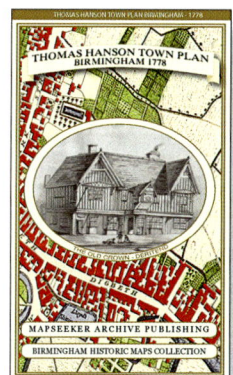

THOMAS HANSON TOWN
PLAN BIRMINGHAM 1778:
ISBN 9781844918096 £14.99

Mapseeker Books – Armchair Time Travellers Series

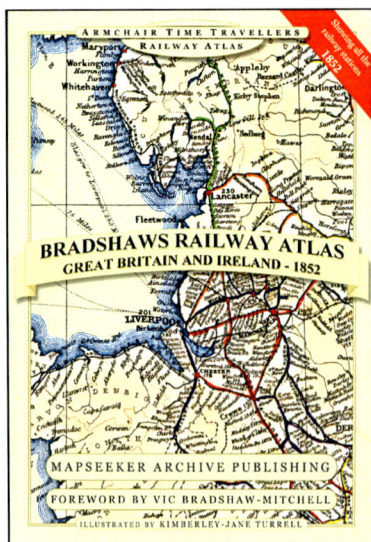

BRADSHAW'S RAILWAY ATLAS OF
GREAT BRITAIN AND IRELAND
Hardcover: ISBN 9781844917914   £29.99
Softcover: ISBN 9781844917907   £19.99

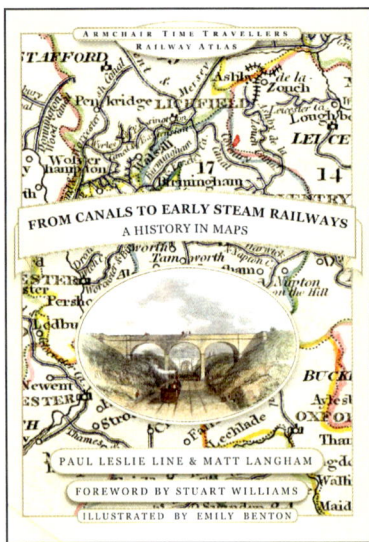

FROM CANALS TO EARLY STEAM RAILWAYS –
A HISTORY IN MAPS
Hardcover: ISBN 9781844917990   £29.99
Softcover: ISBN 9781844917983   £19.99

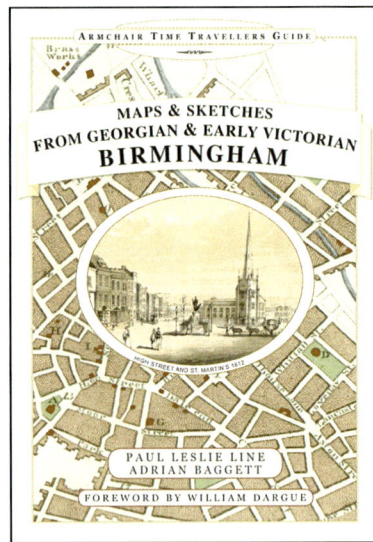

MAPS AND SKETCHES OF GEORGIAN
AND EARLY VICTORIAN BIRMINGHAM
Hardcover: ISBN 9781844918195   £29.99
Softcover: ISBN 9781844918164   £19.99

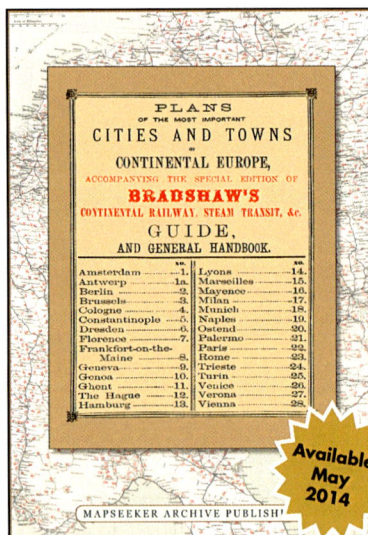

BRADSHAW'S CITIES AND TOWNS PLANS
OF CONTINENTAL EUROPE
Hardcover: ISBN 9781844918003 £19.99

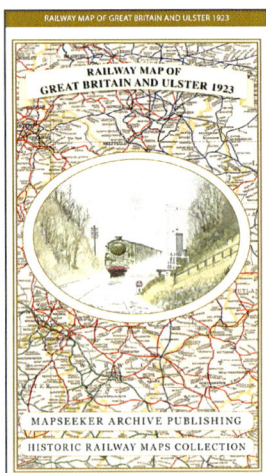

RAILWAY MAP OF GREAT BRITAIN
AND ULSTER 1923:
ISBN 9781844918065 £14.99

BRADSHAW'S RAILWAY MAP –
GREAT BRITAIN AND IRELAND 1852:
ISBN 9781844918041 £14.99

BRADSHAW' RAILWAY MAP –
CENTRAL EUROPE 1913:
ISBN 9781844918058 £14.99

Mapseeker Historic Counties Maps

A COLLECTION OF FOUR
HISTORIC MAPS OF
OXFORDSHIRE
FROM 1611–1836:
ISBN 9781844918140 £19.99

A COLLECTION OF FOUR
HISTORIC MAPS OF
CAMBRIDGESHIRE
FROM 1611–1836:
ISBN 9781844918157 £19.99

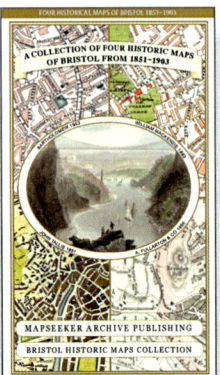

A COLLECTION OF FOUR
HISTORIC MAPS OF
BRISTOL
FROM 1851–1903:
ISBN 9781844918171 £19.99

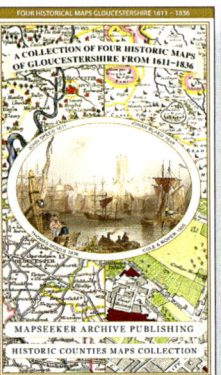

A COLLECTION OF FOUR
HISTORIC MAPS OF
GLOUCESTERSHIRE
FROM 1611–1836:
ISBN 9781844918287 £19.99

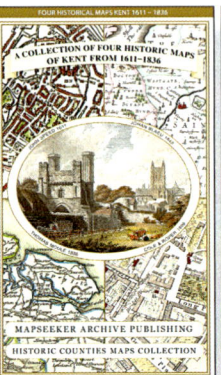

A COLLECTION OF FOUR
HISTORIC MAPS OF
KENT
FROM 1611–1836:
ISBN 9781844918317 £19.99

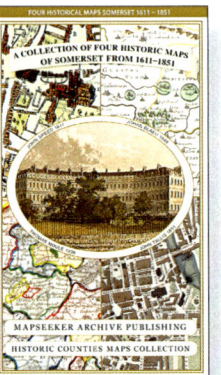

A COLLECTION OF FOUR
HISTORIC MAPS OF
SOMERSET
FROM 1611–1851:
ISBN 9781844918355 £19.99